OUR COUNTRY
AND
ITS PEOPLE

AN INTRODUCTORY GEOGRAPHIC
READER FOR THE FOURTH
SCHOOL YEAR

BY

WILL S. MONROE
STATE NORMAL SCHOOL
MONTCLAIR, NEW JERSEY

AND

ANNA BUCKBEE
STATE NORMAL SCHOOL
CALIFORNIA, PA.

ILLUSTRATED

HARPER & BROTHERS PUBLISHERS
NEW YORK AND LONDON
MCMXI

629079

C

[See page 41

DITCHES FOR PIG-IRON

CONTENTS

ILLUSTRATIONS

PUBLISHERS' NOTE

WE feel certain that teachers and educators generally will recognize the distinctive features of this little book. These have been well stated in the "Foreword to Teachers." But we wish to say a word about the authors and their claims to recognition in the preparation of a work of this kind.

Professor Will S. Monroe is at the head of the department of Psychology and the History of Education in the State Normal School at Montclair, New Jersey. For two years he studied geography with the late Professor Friedrich Ratzel at the University of Leipzig, and Professor Peschel Loesche at Jena. He had charge of the geography classes in the training of teachers at the State Normal School at Westfield, Massachusetts, for twelve years; and he is the author of four successful books of travel and several educational works.

Miss Anna Buckbee has had wide experience as a teacher, superintendent of schools, and educational lecturer. For fifteen years she has been instructor of Pedagogy in the State Normal School at California, Pennsylvania, where she has had extended experience in the use of the oral or Pestalozzian method in teaching geography to children in the primary grades. She is the author of *The Fourth School Year* (Chicago, 1904), one of best worked-out outlines of study for

vii

PUBLISHERS' NOTE

school-children of the age and grade for which "Our Country and Its People" has been prepared. Both Miss Buckbee and Professor Monroe have made important researches in the field of children's geographic interests, and the results of their studies are embodied in this book.

HARPER & BROTHERS.

FOREWORD TO TEACHERS

THE aim of this little volume is to introduce the child to the study of geography from a book. Teachers everywhere recognize the difficulty of making the right connection between the oral instruction of the third grade and the study of the ordinary text-book in the fourth or fifth school year. The more concrete and interesting the oral teaching of the third grade has been, the more keenly the children feel the change to the brief general statements of the primary geography. The authors of this book have tried to make this transition easier and less abrupt for the child by putting into his hands a volume that treats the topic with somewhat the fullness of oral instruction, and, at the same time, is concise enough to serve as the beginning of book study.

Another difficulty encountered by the child when he begins the formal study of geography with a text-book is due to his inability to read the book which is put into his hands. He does not know geographic words, and he meets the twofold problem of learning new words and getting thought from the printed page at the same time. By presenting the subject in the form of simple and interesting reading-lessons, he acquires a vocabulary that facilitates his progress when he begins the formal study of geography with a text-book.

FOREWORD TO TEACHERS

"Our Country and Its People" may be used in any of three ways: (1) As a substitute for the first text-book in geography, the lessons being worked out by the teacher with the class by the aid of wall-maps and whatever illustrative apparatus she may have at hand. (2) It may be used as a geographical reader to supplement the more condensed treatment that primary geographies give of the United States. (3) It will be found especially helpful to those teachers who continue to present geography by means of oral instruction throughout the fourth school year.

One of the authors of this book has had many years' experience with oral instruction in primary schools under the most favorable conditions. She is in entire accord with the advocates of the Pestalozzian method that oral instruction in geography may be made richer and fuller than by the use of any text-book which it is now practicable to supply to all the pupils. But oral instruction makes an unusually heavy demand upon the teacher, unless she has exceptional facilities for preparing the lessons.

The real problem in oral instruction, however, is to keep the mass of material presented to the pupils from fading out of their minds; and the frequent presentation of this difficulty by primary teachers has led to the preparation of this little book. The burden of oral instruction is really upon the child; for he is expected to retain what really amounts to a large book in geography, without any adequate means of review. It is idle to claim that ten-year-old pupils can prepare notes that will be suitable records of what they should retain. Furthermore, it is not fair to restrict the pupils to childish reproductions of lessons as their only permanent records. They have as good right as their

elders to review from a book any subject that they are
required to remember.

The authors hope that teachers will find that the
subjects here presented are organized in such a way
as to offer young children in readable form the essen-
tials of what may have been taught more fully in oral
lessons.

The plan of the book is simple. It brings the child
face to face at once with the fundamental ideas of
geography—that is, the earth as the home of man.
Structure and industries which grow from it, what Nature offers to man and the use he makes of what she
offers, are the keynote of the story. Teachers will
recall that genetic psychologists like Professor Alfred
Binet in France and Professor Earl Barnes in the
United States have pointed out that the dominant
interests of young children are in the use of things—
where and how things are made and what they are
good for. Studies made by the authors of this volume,[1] on the geographic interests of school-children in
Massachusetts and Pennsylvania, show that industrial
activities appeal strongly to the minds of pupils in the
primary grades.

For these reasons it has seemed best to make the
number of topics small and typical, selecting the
largest units of structure and the most closely related
industries. Names of places and political divisions
have been introduced incidentally whenever they
have been needed. It is assumed that in this way

[1] *Geographic Interests and Child Study.* By Anna Buckbee.
American Primary Teacher, December, 1896. Vol. XX.
Die Entwickelung des sozialen Bewusstseins der Kinder.
By Will S. Monroe, Berlin, 1899. (The same translated into
Swedish and Flemish.)

FOREWORD TO TEACHERS

much of what has been called place geography will become familiar to the child in the natural way, just as he learns the names of the streets and buildings in his home town when any interest attaches to them. We believe that this introductory acquaintance will make the later study of political—as well as structural and commercial—geography more pleasant and easy. As already pointed out, a stock of geographic terms and idioms is best acquired in the same way. These have been freely used in the book, sometimes with explanations and sometimes without. In the latter case, it is believed that they can be interpreted by the context, or that, in a few instances, the teacher may need to make the necessary explanation.

THE AUTHORS.

OUR COUNTRY
AND ITS PEOPLE

OUR COUNTRY
AND ITS PEOPLE

I

INTRODUCTION TO THE GEOGRAPHY OF OUR COUNTRY

IT may be that you have not yet begun the study of geography in school, but you already know something about geography. For geography simply tells you about the earth and its people. You live on the earth, and you probably know something about hills, valleys, meadows, marshes, ponds, and streams. You and your family and the folk of your town form a part of the people; and you know something about the things that your part of the earth has to offer for your needs and comforts.

Geography tells about the different parts of the earth, and it tells us what the earth has to offer for the needs and comforts of man. But the earth does not give us all the things that we want ready made and at our doors. Wheat must be grown in the fields. It must be ground into flour at mills. And it must be baked into bread. Cotton must also be grown. It must be spun into yarn, and then it must be woven into cloth before it can be made into clothing. Trees must be sawed into boards, and clay must be molded into bricks before our houses can be built. Coal must be dug from the earth and brought to us before we can burn it.

Not all the things that we need are produced in any one place. Wheat does not grow well in all places. Cotton can be grown only where the summers are long and warm. Trees grow well on the sides of hills and mountains where there is plenty of rain. And most of the coal and other minerals that we need are found in or near mountains. Therefore, many people are engaged in carrying things from one part of the earth to another. Others buy and store the things that are produced until they are needed, and then they sell them again.

So it comes about that nearly all people are engaged in raising something from the earth; in making things so that they may be used; in carrying things about from place to place, or in buying and selling things to others. The land where things are grown is called a farm or plantation. The places where trees are grown are called woods and forests. The places where coal and stone are taken from the earth are called mines and quarries. And the places where cotton and wool are spun into yarn and woven into cloth are called mills and factories.

This book will tell you something about your own country and the things that it produces. It will tell you why some things are grown in one part of the country and taken to another part to be made into useful things. It will tell you what each section of the United States can best produce; where the products are made over—that is, manufactured; where they are carried to, and what and where the great centers of trade are where products are bought and resold.

Mountain ranges and river valleys, soil and rainfall, the skill and the industry of man, and many other things determine what the surface of the earth may be made to yield. You will, therefore, want to know something about the geography of our country, in order to understand why our people produce the things they do.

That is why it is necessary to study about the structure and the climate of the United States. Such study will help you to understand why the cotton that is grown on the coastal plains of the South is taken to New England to be woven into cloth.

You may already know that your country is very large, and that it extends from the Atlantic Ocean on the east to the Pacific Ocean on the west. The distance across the country from New York to San Francisco is about three thousand miles. With an express train it takes from five to six days to make the journey. From north to south our country extends from Canada to Mexico, a distance of about one thousand miles.

Our country is crossed from north to south by two great highlands. Now a highland is

simply land that is elevated or high. It is
made up of mountain ranges and is always
uneven. In the western part of our country
is the Rocky Mountain highland. It is sometimes called the primary highland, because it is
the chief highland in the United States. In
the eastern part of our country is the Appalachian or secondary highland. It is not so
broad or so high as the Rocky Mountain highland, but it is better adapted for human life.

Between these two highlands there is a
broad stretch of land that is low and even. It
is called the central plain of the United States.
There are also broad plains in the southeastern part of our country along the Atlantic
Ocean and the Gulf of Mexico. These lands
are called coastal plains.

The highlands influence our country by
changing the direction of the winds. They
also determine the direction of the rivers.
They make it difficult to build railroads, and
they increase the cost of carrying goods from
one part of the country to another. But they
contain most of the minerals that are useful to
man. Our finest forests are found on the
mountains that form the backbone of the

highlands. And the streams that flow down the slopes of the highlands furnish cheap water-power for our factories and mills.

Our study will begin with the part of the Appalachian highland that is known as the New England upland. This was one of the first parts of our country to be settled by white people, and it is the part that is most thickly settled. Here the soil is not fertile enough to raise big crops, and the land is not level enough to use big farm machinery. But the rivers that flow from the highland give plenty of water-power. The mountains are not high enough to make railroad building difficult. Coal is easily brought from the Allegheny plateau, and transportation is cheap. Here, therefore, we find great factories and mills where cotton and woolen cloth and boots and shoes are made.

In the third lesson we will tell you something about another part of the Appalachian highland that is sometimes called the Allegheny plateau. A plateau is a more or less even part of an elevated region. Highlands are generally made up of several plateaus.

The Allegheny plateau includes parts of the

6

ᔕ a certain part of the Appalachian mountins In western/central New york, N/W. Pennsy N.W. Virginia & east Ohio.

INTRODUCTION

States of Pennsylvania, New York, Maryland, West Virginia, and Ohio. Here we find in the earth two of the chief needs of man—coal to keep him warm, and oil and gas to give him light. Many of the people in this section are occupied in taking these products from the earth and distributing them where they are wanted.

East and south of the Appalachian highland, along the Atlantic Ocean and the Gulf of Mexico, are low and level tracts of land called coastal plains. The States of this region we call the South Atlantic and Gulf States. Here the climate is warm. The soil is fertile. Rainfall is abundant. Many industries might be carried on here. But the people of the coastal plains have learned that it pays to produce the things that are wanted and that cannot be raised elsewhere; and they have engaged in growing cotton, sugar, and rice.

We have already mentioned the low, smooth region between the Appalachian and the Rocky Mountain highlands. This region is known as the central lowlands of the United States; and the lower parts in the upper Mississippi Valley are called prairies. This section is the "bread basket" for the people who toil in factories and mines or labor on cotton and sugar plantations. The growing of wheat and corn are the leading industries of the people of the prairies. Nature has given them smooth fields and rich soil, and they have been skilful and industrious in the cultivation of wheat, corn, and other grains.

The Great Lakes, which are northeast of the prairies, are fine, natural waterways for trade and commerce, and they supply us with fine fresh-water fish.

Between the prairies and the Rocky Mountain highland there are great stretches of gently sloping land that we call the Western plains. They are really the foot-hills of the Rocky Mountains. Here are the great pasture lands of the United States. The westerly winds that come from the Pacific Ocean lose their moisture in crossing the high ridges of the Sierra Nevadas and the broad plateaus of the Rocky Mountain highland. The rainfall is so slight that grains can be grown only where the land can be irrigated—that is, where water can be taken from streams and caused to flow over the land. But grass grows easily on the Western plains, and millions of cattle and sheep are raised. The meat is sent as food to the people of other parts of our country, and the hides are sent to New England to be made into boots and shoes.

West of the Rocky Mountain highland, between the Sierra Nevada Mountains and the low coast range that runs along the edge of the land that borders the Pacific Ocean, are several long and narrow valleys. One of these is the beautiful California Valley, where the people grow oranges, lemons, grapes, and many other kinds of fruit.

In the lessons that follow, a chapter will be given to each of these sections of our country, and you will learn how and why the people of the United States are engaged in producing the things from the earth that are needed for their comforts. If you understand these lessons, by the time you have finished the book you will know a good deal about the geography of our country and its people.

Some Points to Remember

1. Geography tells us about the earth and what it produces for our needs and comforts.

2. Not all the things that are needed are produced in any one place, therefore some things must be made and carried to other parts.

3. The structure and the climate of a country influence the occupation of the people.

4. The United States is so large that its structure and climate differ in different parts.

5. Two highlands cross our country from north to south.

6. Between these highlands are the broad and low central plains.

II.—THE NEW ENGLAND UPLAND

IN the first lesson you read about highlands and lowlands. Now an upland is simply a high tract of land. The New England upland, however, is not so high as most of the highlands in our country. It is a worn-out mountain range that has been slowly worn down until only the base of the mountains remain. The upland occupies the northeastern part of our country. It includes the six small States of Maine, New Hampshire, Vermont, Massachusetts, Rhode Island, and Connecticut.

The highest part of the upland is in the north, where we find the White Mountains of New Hampshire and the Green Mountains of Vermont. It reaches elevations of from 1,500 to 2,000 feet, and slopes gently to the south and east. There are a number of deep and narrow river valleys in the highland.

The White Mountains are composed of irregular groups of ranges and peaks, some of which rise a mile or more above the level of the sea. The highest group is called the Presidential range, because its peaks have been named for some of the early Presidents of the United States. Mount Washington is more than a mile high; and Mount Adams, Mount Jefferson, Mount Madison, and Mount Monroe are all nearly as high.

Many rivers take their rise in the northern part of the highland. The longest of these are the Connecticut, the Penobscot, and the Kennebec. They have cut channels in the surface of the upland, where the rocks are weak or soft. The main rivers of the upland are fed by many smaller streams, for the New England States are well watered. The annual rainfall for this section is from thirty-five to fifty inches.

The New England highland was once much higher and more rugged than it is to-day. But the sharp ridges and the high peaks were worn off a long time ago by the action of great ice sheets, called glaciers. The highland was once covered by a mass of thick ice much as Greenland is to-day. It came from the North and crept slowly down the slope of the upland toward the ocean. As it moved along it scraped from the surface the loose soil and it plucked from their ledges many large rocks which it carried for miles.

Because of some change in the climate, the glacier finally disappeared; but there was left spread over the upland the mass of gravel and stones that the ice sheet had brought from the North. Some of the large rocks had been rounded and worn smooth by rubbing against other stones. Such glacial-worn rocks are called boulders, and the New England upland is strewn with them.

There was also scattered over the land, as the ice sheet melted, fine material known as boulder clay or till; and on the lower edges of the ice sheet, where the boulder clay was abundant, great mounds were formed. These mounds, or rounded hills, are called drumlins. In the southern part of the New England upland, near the ocean, hundreds of drumlins may be seen.

Rivers were turned from their courses by heaps of material deposited by the melting glacier. In the same way many beautiful lakes were formed. Some of the streams thus changed from their courses have worn down soft rocks and deepened the valleys, and others tumble over the ledges of hard rocks that are not so easily worn down by the action of the water. Such waterfalls, before the introduction of steam and electricity, furnished the power for the cotton and the woolen mills and the boot and shoe factories.

The winters in the northern part of the New England highland are very cold, and the rivers are frozen over for three or four months of the year. The ice on the streams and lakes is sometimes more than two feet thick, and ice-cutting furnishes employment to many men during the winter months. Storms are frequent in New England, and the weather often changes several times a day. The summers are hot; and, as you have already been told, the rainfall is heavy. There is always a great deal of moisture in the air, but the moisture aids greatly in the spinning of cotton cloth, which is one of the chief industries of the upland.

THE NEW ENGLAND UPLAND

The highest part of the upland being in the north, the short and abrupt slope is toward the St. Lawrence River, and the long and gradual slope is toward the Atlantic Ocean. The coastal part of the upland has sunk; and at the mouth of each river, as it enters the sea, there is a sheltered bay that forms a harbor. These bays are really drowned valleys; and many of the small islands along the New England coast are half-drowned hills.

The New England upland consists of rock masses of many different kinds. Some of these, such as granite, marble, and limestone, are very useful to man. Granite is very abundant, very hard, and very strong; and great quantities of granite slabs are shipped from the quarries near Rutland, in Vermont, Quincy, in Massachusetts, and Westerly, in Rhode Island. Vermont is famous for its marble, and the Connecticut Valley for its sandstone.

The area of New England is only one-fortieth that of the United States, but it has one-fifteenth of the population of the country. Rhode Island and Massachusetts are the most thickly populated States in our country. This is because they contain so many factory towns, and because the New England upland was one of the parts of our country that was first settled by white men.

The upland was settled nearly three hundred years ago by people who came from England. So long as the number of people was not great, they engaged in farming on small tracts of fertile land in the river valleys and on the lower parts of the upland near the sea.

As you have already been told, most of the soil of New England is not very good. The great glacier, that we have already told you about, buried much of the rich surface loam, and it scattered gravel and boulders over the upland. So as the number of people grew, they engaged more and more in the manufacture of cotton and woolen cloth and boots and shoes.

In the fourth lesson you will read about the coastal plains of our country and the great plantations where cotton is grown. In the present lesson we will tell you something about the mills where the cotton is woven into cloth. The soil of New England is too poor and the summers are too short for the growth of cotton; but there are in the upland more than forty large towns engaged in the manufacture of calico, gingham, sheeting, and other kinds of cotton cloth. Some of the largest cotton-mills in the world are at Fall River and Lowell, in Massachusetts, Pawtucket, in Rhode Island, and Manchester, in New Hampshire.

Most of the cloth for our clothing is made from the hair of animals or the fiber of plants. By fiber is meant the thin and delicate threads. Cotton comes from a plant fiber. The cotton plant belongs to the mallow family, and it is a near relative of the common hollyhock that you may have seen growing in a yard or garden. But the fourth lesson will tell you how cotton is grown; and, if you would like to know the story of its growth at once, you may turn to that chapter and read about the low coastal plains and the great cotton plantations.

After the cotton has been picked in the fields of the South, it is packed into bales and shipped to the mills and factories of New England. It is cleaned, and arranged in laps or rolls; for the mass of cotton in the bales is composed of very thin fibers from half an inch to an inch and a half in length. The tangled mass is straightened out, and the very short fibers are removed. This is called carding the cotton. The fibers are then spun into threads. In the spinning two or more fibers of the cotton are combined into a single cord. A pound of cotton fiber may be spun into thread so fine that it will reach from New York to Chicago, which is a distance of one thousand miles.

In the olden time, cotton was spun into thread by hand. This was done by the unmarried women in families, hence our word spinster for unmarried or single women. But to-day the slender cotton fibers are drawn into threads on rods, called spindles, by machinery; and each cotton-mill in New England has thousands of spindles operated by machines. Some of the mills merely card the cotton fiber and spin it into thread, and send the thread to factories to be woven into cloth. But at some of the mills the carding and spinning, as well as the weaving, is done.

Many years ago cotton cloth was woven by hand in great wooden looms. To-day the thread is woven into fabrics in looms that are operated by machinery. Threads are first

18

placed lengthwise in the looms. These are crossed by other threads. The long threads are called the warp; and the short ones, that cross them, the woof or welt. The interlacing of the thread forms the cloth. The thread of the woof is passed from one side of the loom to the other, between the threads of the warp, by means of a shuttle.

All this is done by machinery. One girl can attend to hundreds of spindles, where the cotton is spun into thread; and a man can attend to two great looms, where the thread is woven into calico, gingham, and sheeting. There are in our country twenty-two million spindles for the spinning of cotton thread, and half a million looms for the manufacture of cotton cloth.

Formerly all the cotton cloth made in our country came from New England; but in recent times some of the States of the South, and particularly North Carolina, have built cotton-mills. Fall River, in Massachusetts, sometimes called "the Cotton City of America," weaves great quantities of calico, gingham, and sheeting. It is located on the Narragansett River, near where that stream falls from the lowest part of the upland to tide-level; and this gave the town great advantage when cotton - mills were driven entirely by water - power. Lowell, New Bedford, Lawrence, and other Massachusetts towns weave quantities of cotton cloth; and Pawtucket, in Rhode Island, and Manchester, in New Hampshire, are also important cotton towns.

More cotton cloth is made in the United States than in any other country. We make the plainer and cheaper grades of goods, and we use most of the cotton cloth that we manufacture. The finer and more expensive cotton fabrics we buy from England, France, Germany, Belgium, and Switzerland.

There are also in New England many factories for the manufacture of woolen cloth, worsted goods, and carpets. These fabrics are made from the hair of animals, usually sheep, but sometimes the hair of goats and alpacas is used. In a later lesson on the great plains of the West you will be told about the raising of sheep. After the wool has been sheared from the backs of the sheep, it is shipped to the factories, where it is sorted so as to put the different threads together. Then it is washed in lye and clean water to get the grease out of it. . The dust is blown from it, and it is picked over by hand to remove the knots. Then the fiber is spun into yarn.

In making yarn for woolen cloth, the wool is simply spun into loose thread. But in making yarn for worsteds, the wool is combed and twisted until the thread becomes hard. The cloth is then made in great looms that are very much like the looms used in the making of cotton cloth. After the cloth is woven, it is beaten in water and soap with wooden mallets or hammers that the oil and dirt may be gotten out. After this it is washed; and if it is to be colored cloth, and the yarn has not already been dyed, it is now dyed in the piece. It is washed again and stretched upon frames to dry.

Again it is soaked in water and pounded or rolled, in order that the fibers may felt together. This causes the cloth to shrink very much, but it becomes thicker. The cloth is then pressed, folded, and packed, and is ready to be sold. You must have already noted that the task of making woolen is much greater than that of making cotton cloth, and

you will also remember that woolen cloth
costs much more than cotton cloth, and that
woolen clothes keep you much warmer in
winter than cotton clothes.

The chief woolen fabrics made in New England are woolen cloth, worsteds, and carpets.
The yarn for the woolen cloth is only slightly
twisted, and the fibers are crossed in every
way, so as to leave them free for felting. But
for worsteds, the fibers of the wool are all
laid out straight, and the threads of the yarn
are twisted until they become very hard. If
you will compare a piece of woolen cloth with a
piece of worsted you will notice at once the
difference in the two kinds of fabrics.

Massachusetts ranks first in our country in
the manufacture of woolen cloth and worsteds,
and third in carpet. Rhode Island ranks
second; and considerable woolen cloth is
made in Maine, Connecticut, and New Hampshire. The great woolen cities of New England are Providence, Lawrence, Pittsfield,
Lowell, Fitchburg, and Woonsocket; and
carpets are made at Worcester and Clinton.
Perhaps you will want to find on a map the
location of each of these towns. Other States

in our country that make woolen fabrics are
New York, Pennsylvania, and New Jersey.

Boots and shoes are made in one hundred
and fifty towns in New England; but in the
three towns of Lynn, Brockton, and Haver-
hill—all in Massachusetts—two-thirds of the
shoes of our country are produced. You
probably know that boots and shoes are made
from the hides of animals; and in a later
lesson on the Western plains you will read
about the cattle that are raised for their meat
and hides and tallow. The raw skins of
animals are called hides; and most of the hides
used in the making of boots and shoes come
from cattle. Some hides also come from
sheep, goats, horses, kangaroos, and alligators.

After the skins have been taken from the
animals they must be tanned; that is, they
must be soaked in the ground bark of hemlock
or oak trees. Long ago it was found that the
tanning of skins hardened them and made
them wear well. The hides are soaked in the
ground bark and other tanning stuff for a couple of weeks, and then they are washed and
dried. Tanned hides are called leather. The
leather is again hardened by being hammered

or rolled under heavy steel rollers. The part
of the leather to be used for the uppers of the
shoes is split and rubbed with oil or tallow.

The making of the shoe begins by cutting
the different parts from the leather, as the
uppers, the soles, and the heels. There are a
number of different pieces to the uppers.
The part that fits about the ankle is called the
large quarter. The part that covers the front
of the foot is called the vamp. The uppers
and soles are cut from the leather by hand by a
cutter with a pattern and a sharp knife, and
the heels are cut with a die or steel punch.

The next step in the making of a shoe is to
sew the different parts together. This was
formerly done by hand, and it took a shoe-
maker several days to make a pair of shoes.
To-day it is done by sewing-machines, and a
pair of shoes may be made in fifteen or twenty
minutes. The various parts of the uppers are
first sewed together, and then the soles and
the uppers are joined by means of sewing-
machines. Even the heels are fastened to the
shoe by machinery; and the nails that are
used are cut from steel wire and driven into
the heels at the same time. The cutting of the

24

MAKING BOOTS AND SHOES IN NEW ENGLAND

parts of the shoe is done largely by men; but the sewing-machines are operated by women and girls. One woman can sew from seven to eight hundred pairs of shoes a day.

More boots and shoes are made in the United States than in any other country; and while most of the American boots and shoes are made in New England, there are large factories in New York City, Rochester, Philadelphia, Chicago, and St. Louis. We make so many boots and shoes that we are not only able to supply the needs of our own people, but we also sell great quantities to the people of the old world.

England, Germany, and France also make many boots and shoes, for most people of the world to-day wear covering for the feet made of leather. This was not always so. In ancient Egypt, a very old country in northern Africa, about which you will study in geography, the people wore sandals made of palm leaves. Now a sandal is simply a sole that is fastened to the foot with straps.

Indians wore moccasins made of deerskin, or other soft leather. In Japan and China shoes are still made of straw, and in Holland,

Belgium, and some other parts of Europe, many of the people wear shoes that are cut from blocks of wood. The wooden shoes worn by the peasants, or common people of Europe, are called sabots. They keep the feet warm and dry, but they make a great clatter in walking.

This finishes our story of the New England upland and its industries. We have not told you about all the things that the people of the New England States make for their needs and comforts, as well as for the needs and comforts of others, but we have told you about the principal things.

Later in your course, when you study the geography of this section, you will learn about the manufacture of paper, the products of the forests, and the fisheries on the coast. For the present, it is enough that you should know something about the nature of the highland and its chief industries, which are the making of cotton and woolen cloth and boots and shoes.

Some Points to Remember

1. The New England upland is a highland, but it is not so high as most of the other highlands in our country.

2. The highland is composed of irregular groups of mountain ranges and peaks.

3. The highest peak in the upland is Mount Washington, which is 6,293 feet above the level of the sea.

4. The highest part of the upland is in the north, and the long slope is toward the east and the south.

5. The principal rivers of New England are the Connecticut, the Penobscot, and the Kennebec.

6. Rainfall is abundant, and lakes and streams are numerous.

7. The slope of the upland and the numerous streams furnish cheap water-power for mills and factories.

8. The weaving of cotton and woolen cloth and the making of boots and shoes are the principal occupations of the people of New England.

III.—THE ALLEGHENY PLATEAU

A GREAT highland extends through the eastern part of North America from the Gulf of St. Lawrence to South Carolina. It is called the Appalachian highland; and the New England upland, about which you read in the last lesson, is simply a part of this elevated region. In this lesson you will learn some things about the central part of the Appalachian highland and the useful minerals that are found in its rocky layers.

In the eastern part of the Appalachian highland we find the worn and rounded Blue Ridge Mountains, and in the western part the broad Allegheny and Cumberland plateaus. Between the Blue Ridge Mountains and the plateaus there is a long and narrow depression that is not so elevated as the eastern ridges and much lower than the western plateaus. This depression is called the Great Valley. Most of the rivers of the highland take their rise in the plateaus. They cross the Great Valley and reach the Atlantic Ocean through water-gaps in the Blue-Ridge Mountains.

The southern part of the Appalachian highland is broader and higher than the central part. Here we find Mount Mitchell, the highest peak in the eastern part of our country. In the Cumberland plateau the mountains contain coal and iron, and the slopes of the plateau are well wooded.

But in this lesson you are to learn about only one division of the Appalachian highland, the Allegheny plateau. It includes the southern and western parts of New York, the western part of Pennsylvania, and parts of Ohio, West Virginia, and Maryland. The average elevation of the plateau is about a thousand feet. On the eastern side the plateau slopes abruptly to the Great Valley, but the western slopes descend gradually to the prairies and the Gulf coastal plain. The Allegheny plateau contains rich mines of useful minerals, such as coal, iron, petroleum, and natural gas.

In the early days of our country—that is, before canals, railroads, and steamboats had become common—the mining of coal was a very simple matter. Any one who needed it, in the region where it lay close to the surface, had only to go to the nearest outcropping with a pick and shovel. He broke loose what he needed; shoveled it into a basket, a bag, or a cart, and took it to his home or shop. There was little trade in coal in those days, because it was too heavy to carry long distances by any of the means of transportation then in use. To-day all that is changed, and many people are engaged in mining coal and carrying it to places where it is needed.

Coal is spread out in layers in the earth. These layers are sometimes called seams, sometimes veins, and sometimes simply beds of coal. In the United States coal occupies about two hundred thousand square miles. Now that is a very large area. It is more than four times the size of the State of New York; and two-thirds of our coal is found in three States in the Allegheny plateau—Pennsylvania, West Virginia, and Ohio.

The coal veins vary in thickness from a few inches to thirty or more feet. In many places they are fairly level. This makes it very convenient for handling the coal. In other places the beds lie slanting in the earth, when they are said to dip. The veins of hard coal in eastern Pennsylvania are often folded and twisted in such a way as to make the work of mining very difficult indeed.

When layers of coal come to the surface, they are said to outcrop. These outcrops may often be seen in the bluffs along the river valleys and at places where the railroads have made cuttings. In some of the coal regions, however, the miners must go down as far as fifteen hundred feet to find the coal.

The hardest coal is called anthracite, and is found mainly in eastern Pennsylvania. A softer coal is found along the western slopes of the Allegheny plateau and in the Mississippi Valley that is called bituminous coal. Our country mines nearly four times as much bituminous as anthracite coal.

Coal is sometimes procured by merely uncovering the beds where it is near the surface and taking it out somewhat as stone is quarried. This is called stripping. Sometimes large veins of coal lie not far below the surface. These are called drifts; and if the coal outcrops above a valley or stream, all that has to be done is to drive a tunnel up into the seam.

Another kind of coal-mine is the slope. In this the coal veins slant downward. A tunnel is driven down to the vein and the coal is brought up to the surface. Most of the coal is so deep in the earth that it can only be reached by sinking a shaft.

Since the days of the man with the pick and shovel and basket, three things have greatly increased the demand for coal. One is the increased use that is made of coal in factories, engines, and for heating purposes in our homes. Another is the improvements that have been made in transporting coal from the mines to the places where it is needed. A third is the invention of machines that mine and handle the coal cheaply.

All these changes act one upon another in a sort of a circle, something after the manner of the story in the rhyme that tells about "The

House that Jack Built." The coal enables
the mills to make iron and steel. Iron and
steel are used to build railroads to carry coal
to mills that will make more iron and steel to
build more railroads. More coal must be
mined for the new mills that make the iron
and steel for the new railroads, and so on.

You have already been told that most of the
coal is taken from the mines by a shaft sunk
into the earth. Now a shaft is much like a
large well or a deep cellar. The sides must be
strongly braced with timber so that they will
not cave in. The usual size of a mine shaft
is twelve feet by thirty. Partitions divide the
shaft crosswise into four compartments. One
of the compartments is used for pumping the
water from the mine. Another is used to
ventilate the mine—that is, to force fresh air
in and foul gases and bad air out. The other
two compartments are used to take the men
and mules and coal cars down into the mine
and to bring them out again.

At the foot of the shaft a straight passage
or tunnel is driven for some distance into the
coal vein. This is extended as the work continues, and is called the main entry or gang-

33

way. From this a side passage branches off at right angles. Other passages are dug, and all are connected with the air-passage of the main shaft; for at the top of the shaft is a great fan that sucks the foul gases and bad air from the passages and allows fresh air to take their place. It is very necessary that the miners should have a constant supply of good air.

You doubtless know that under the surface of the earth there are always small streams of water. Now these streams would soon flood the mine if the water was not constantly pumped to the surface. You have also read that one of the compartments of the mine shaft is for this purpose.

Having told you something of the ventilation and the drainage of a mine, we are now ready to tell you of the actual work of mining the coal. The main entry from the bottom of the shaft, that we have already mentioned, is extended; side entries are dug; and from the side entries passages are cut at right angles running parallel with the main entry. Perhaps you will take a piece of paper and pencil and make a drawing of these entries and passages. Or, if you will imagine the streets of an underground city, you will get some notion of the appearance of a coal - mine. Blocks or pillars of coal must be left standing that the roof may be held up.

There are three ways of loosening the coal in the vein—by using a pick, by drilling and blasting, and by cutting with a machine. Machines that are run by electricity or compressed air cut the coal from the beds into great blocks as easily as you would cut a loaf of bread into slices with a sharp knife.

One of the difficult problems in mining is how to keep the roof from falling; for the pillars of coal left standing are not strong enough to support the weight of rock above. Miners, therefore, put in great numbers of hardwood posts as supports. But, in spite of all the care that is taken, many miners are killed every year by the falling of slate and rock.

Miners are often killed or injured by the explosive gases that are set free in mining the coal. These gases collect near the roof; and, as the miners come along with lighted lamps in their caps, the gas takes fire and serious injuries often result. Fires often take place

4   35

as the result of such explosions; and other dangers have to be faced by the men who dig the coal from the mines that warms our homes and furnishes the power for our engines and factories.

After the coal has been loosened from the earth by picks, blasting, or machinery, it must be taken to the bottom of the shaft on small cars that are drawn by mules; then it is lifted to the surface, much as you may have seen a large box taken by an elevator from the ground floor to one of the upper stories of a high building. In the case of hard or anthracite coal, after it is brought from the mine it must be taken to a breaker to be broken up.

After coal has been broken into pieces of different sizes by machinery, it is then made to pass through a series of sieves, which sort it into several sizes. These different sizes give the name to the different kinds of hard coal as we find them in the market. Some of these names are lump coal, egg coal, large stove coal, small stove coal, chestnut coal, and pea coal.

Quantities of soft or bituminous coal mined in the Allegheny plateau are made into coke before being used as fuel. Coke is made by

36

burning soft coal in an oven. These ovens are made of brick and are cone-shaped inside. There are openings at the top to put the coal in, and doors at the side from which to draw the coke out.

After the coal has been allowed to burn slowly for forty-eight hours or more, water is turned in to cool it off, and the coke is removed from the oven and shipped where it is needed. Most coke is used in iron and steel mills in melting the ore and pig-iron. It is also used by blacksmiths and by railroads for locomotives, and sometimes it is used in furnaces for heating houses.

The use of iron by man is very old. How old we do not know. It is probable that the first iron-makers were savages who built a fire upon a rock that contained iron ore. When the fire went out, they found that the partly melted rock could be pounded into better-shaped weapons and tools than those they had made from stone. Somehow they learned that if they heated the iron-bearing rock until it melted it would separate from the other materials mixed with it. But it was not easy to melt it.

Primitive men had learned that a draught made their fires burn better; so they piled broken ore and wood between high rocks, so that the wind might rush through. Later it was discovered that if limestone was put into the pile the impurities of the ore would stick to the lime and form a scum, just as happens when your mother boils fruit and sugar together.

Finally, one day, some one thought to build a chimney over his heap of ore. He found that he had a good draught without depending upon the wind. When the melted ore was cooled a little, he hammered it into shape. Thus was completed the necessary steps in making iron from the ore that is found in the earth mixed with rocks. Iron was known in the time of Homer, the blind old Greek poet, and he lived a very long time ago.

But you want to know about the iron and steel industry in your own country; where the ore is found; how and where it is made into steel. We have already told you that the Allegheny plateau has many mills for making iron ore into steel, and the steel into steel plate, steel rails, locomotives, machinery, and many other things that are made of iron.

Pure iron is never found in the earth without being mixed with something else. Certain sands, gravel, and rocks contain iron and other minerals. If they contain considerable iron, we call them iron ores. Now, iron ore is found in nearly all parts of the earth; but some ores are much richer than others. Minnesota and Michigan have the richest iron ores in our country. Alabama, Virginia, Tennessee, and Pennsylvania come next. And we import much iron ore from Cuba.

Iron is mined much as coal is. Some of the ore is so near the surface that it may be loosened with steam-shovels and loaded into cars or boats. Some of it is blasted from the earth as is done with coal. Some iron-mines are worked as a drift; others as a slope; and in still others a shaft is sunk into the earth and the ore is hoisted to the surface.

Iron ore is very heavy; but the same is true of the coal and limestone that are needed for smelting it—that is, separating the rocky parts from the true iron by heating. We find, therefore, the iron-mills near the coal-mines.

And since you already know that the Allegheny region is the great coal-bin of our country, you will look for the mills in the parts of the plateau where there are good waterways and railways. Pittsburg meets these requirements, and it is the great center of the iron and steel industries in our country; although you will find such mills in most parts of the Appalachian highland south of the New England upland, and particularly in the Cumberland plateau.

Now that you have learned where the ore comes from and where the mills are located, you will want to know how the iron is made ready for use. You have already read that the first process is called smelting. This is done at a blast-furnace. Now, a furnace is not a building, but a huge steel cylinder, lined with fire-brick, and towering eighty or more feet in the air. At the bottom is a sort of tank called the hearth. ·Air-pipes enter just above the hearth, for it is the blast of air that feeds the fire and causes the ore to melt.

The furnace is filled from the top with ore, coke, and limestone. As the mass melts, the impurities separate from the iron. As the iron is much heavier than the impurities, it sinks to the bottom and is taken from the furnace by a door at the bottom of the hearth. As it leaves the furnace it is a red-hot stream. The limestone, coke ashes, and other impurities, being much lighter than the mass of pure iron, they are taken from the furnace by a door at the top of the hearth.

The streams of red-hot iron are run into little ditches that are filled with sand. Here the iron cools, and the cooled pieces are called pig-iron. But the pig-iron must again be melted and refined and made into what is called wrought iron or steel. Pig-iron might be compared to the yarn that is made from the raw cotton and wool that you read about in the lesson on the New England upland. You learned that the cotton yarn must be woven into cloth, and the cloth made into clothing. So the pig-iron must be worked over into malleable iron—that is, iron which can be easily hammered into different shapes —and steel before it can be made into tools and machines and rails and engines and other useful things.

Many of our useful iron products are made

from steel, a very hard kind of iron. There is no such thing as a steel ore. The pig-iron is changed into steel by being heated with a mixture of charcoal, or by melting it and driving a blast of air through it. Steel is used for knives, tools, rails, machines, and many other things; and in different parts of the Allegheny region there are great factories where all kinds of steel and iron products are made for the use and comfort of man. Try and recall all the things in your home that are made of iron and steel; and then make a list of the different uses of iron and steel in your town.

Sixty years ago people used candles and lamps filled with lard or whale-oil to light their homes. But these gave so little light that it was not easy to read or sew in the evening; and cars and churches were very dimly lighted. And the streets of the cities and towns were very dark after nightfall.

For a long time the people who lived on the western slopes of the Allegheny plateau had noticed on the surface of springs and pools of water a dark kind of oil; but they used it only as medicine. Finally some men in Pittsburg found that with a glass chimney this oil could be used for lighting their houses.

As the oil had always been found on springs and streams of water, men finally bored holes in the earth and discovered great pools of oil. In order to reach the oil a hole has to be dug into the earth for a long distance. Sometimes men have to dig down a half-mile before they reach the oil-pool.

In some wells the oil does not have to be pumped out. The pressure is so great that it flows out, much as you may have seen water shoot into the air in a fountain. These are called artesian wells. A pipe is attached to the top of the well to save the oil. The pipes run into great steel tanks that hold thousands of gallons.

Sometimes the oil-tanks take fire. A burning oil-tank is an awful spectacle. Great clouds of black smoke are carried into the air and spread over the country; and if the burning oil should flow down a narrow valley—as it sometimes does—it causes great destruction.

When the oil comes from the well, it is thick and has a dirty yellowish color. This is the crude oil. But such oil does not burn well

43

in lamps. It must be refined. So it is taken from the great tanks in iron pipes to the refineries. One oil company has four thousand miles of oil-pipes. That is, if its oil-pipes were placed end to end, they would reach from San Francisco to New York, and from New York again west as far as Chicago. Sometimes the oil is carried to the refineries in tank-cars.

At the refineries, the crude oil is distilled—that is, the impurities are removed. The crude oil is heated in great boilers. The vapor that comes from the heating is carried through tubes that are kept in cold water. This causes the moisture in the air to collect much as damp air will collect on the outside of a pitcher of cold water that is brought into a warm room. The thinnest and lightest liquid collects first. This makes the naphtha that we use in varnish and for other purposes. The next thinnest is the gasoline that is much used to-day by automobiles. Then comes the benzine that we use for cleaning purposes. Finally there is condensed the kerosene that we burn in lamps.

There remains in the boilers a thick, heavy mass that looks like dirty molasses. From this coal-tar, machine oil, dyes for coloring cloth, and wax for candles and chewing-gum are made.

Another quite wonderful mineral product of the Allegheny plateau is natural gas. It is usually found in connection with petroleum. Wells are drilled into the earth in much the same way as the oil-wells. When a reservoir of gas is tapped it rushes to the surface ready to be used in lighting streets, warming homes, and cooking meals. All that needs to be done is to pipe it to the towns where it is needed. Some pipes carry gas to towns that are two hundred and fifty miles from the wells.

Natural gas is used chiefly for lighting and heating buildings. It is cheap; it gives a brilliant light, and it burns without smoke or ashes. In many homes on the Allegheny plateau there are no lamps or coal-bins to fill, and no ashes to be removed. The people who use natural gas simply strike a match, turn on the gas, and their fires are ready.

Some Points to Remember

1. The Allegheny plateau is in the west central part of the Appalachian highland.

2. It includes the southern and western part

of New York, the western part of Pennsylvania, and parts of West Virginia, Ohio, and Maryland.

3. It contains in great quantities four very useful mineral products—coal, iron, petroleum, and natural gas.

4. Coal is found in the earth in veins, seams, or beds. Most of it is mined by sinking shafts into the earth.

5. The hard coal is called anthracite and the soft coal bituminous.

6. Quantities of bituminous coal are used in the manufacture of coke.

7. Coal is necessary for the manufacture of iron ore into steel and machinery, hence the large number of furnaces and steel-mills in the Allegheny plateau.

8. Some of the largest oil-wells in our country are found in the Allegheny plateau.

9. Great reservoirs of natural gas are found in the neighborhood of petroleum.

IV.—THE COASTAL PLAINS

COTTON-FIELDS AND SUGAR-PLANTATIONS

FROM New York to Texas there are low,
flat plains that border the Atlantic Ocean
and the Gulf of Mexico. They are called
coastal plains and they contain some rich
agricultural lands. The surface is level; the
soil is everywhere deep; the climate is very
moderate, and the rainfall is abundant. These
are the conditions that favor the growth of
cotton and sugar-cane.

The coastal plains of our country include
portions of the Carolinas, Georgia, Alabama,
Mississippi, and Texas, and all of Florida and
Louisiana. The higher ground between the
Atlantic coastal plain and the Appalachian
highland is called the Piedmont belt. It
grows some cotton, but its chief crops are
tobacco and corn.

More than six hundred years ago a famous

traveler, Marco Polo by name, came home to Venice after a journey of twenty years in Asia. He wrote a book in which he told about the wonderful things that he had seen; and one of the marvels that he described was the growth of wool on trees. What he had really seen was the cotton-plant. It is no longer a matter of wonder, since much cloth is to-day made from cotton, and cotton-plantations are found in most warm countries.

When our country was settled, nearly three hundred years ago, people had learned how to make cloth from the cotton-plant; and very early in the history of our country, it was found that cotton could be grown in Virginia and other parts of the Atlantic coastal plain. It was not, however, until after the invention of the cotton-gin and the steamboat that the growth of cotton became an important industry.

Cotton grows on small trees, bushes, vines, and on low plants called herbs. Tree cotton is found in India, but is not cultivated for the market. Bush cotton is also found in India, and is cultivated for the fiber that is used for making a kind of cloth called Madras and the

PICKING COTTON IN THE SOUTH

beautiful India muslins. The cotton that is grown on the Atlantic and Gulf coastal plains of our country comes from an herb.

Two kinds of cotton are grown in our country—sea-island cotton and upland cotton. Sea-island cotton is grown on the islands and low coastal plains of South Carolina, Georgia, and Florida. It produces a longer and finer fiber than upland cotton and is much used for making thread.

Upland cotton is much more widely grown and is produced in large quantities on the Piedmont belt and the Gulf coastal plain. Texas produces the most. But nearly all of the States of the Atlantic and Gulf coastal plains produce large quantities of upland cotton.

The seed must be sown in the spring and the crop gathered in the autumn. The date for planting varies. Near the coast it may take place as early as the first of March; but in the upland regions of the Piedmont belt, the ground is not warm enough until the end of April.

The preparation of the ground requires a great deal of work. It must first be broken

49

with a plow. Then it must be worked over with a fine harrow. Then it must be bedded up into ridges about four feet apart. After all danger of frost has passed the seed is planted in the ridges by a machine that is something like a corn-planter.

When the young plants get four leaves, the rows must be thinned, since the machine sows too many seed. This is done by hand by patient colored people. The blossoms come in July or August, and they are very beautiful. When they first appear they are cream-colored but they soon grow pink and red. In three or four days they fall off and a tiny pod appears where the blossom was. This pod is called the boll, and it continues to grow until it becomes as large as a hen's egg. The boll has from three to six apartments or cells which contain seeds wrapped in the soft white downy substance that we call the cotton fiber or lint.

When the seed is ripe the bolls burst open and the cotton stalks are covered with white fluffy balls. A ripe cotton-field is a beautiful sight; and if the crop is a large one, the planter, as the cotton farmer is called, is very happy. For there is much hard work for the planter

and his help and a good deal of anxiety. If
there happens to be a late frost, the plants are
killed or injured. If there happens to be a
long season without rain, or too much rain,
the plants do not produce good cotton. And
then there are many plant diseases and insect
pests that may injure the plant.

Picking the cotton is the most interesting
part of the work; and it is all done by hand.
It is not hard work, and the women and the
children help the men. The pickers walk
between the rows and pick the mass of fibers—
or lint, as the planters call it—from the bolls,
and put it into sacks or bags which they carry.
These sacks or bags are emptied into large
baskets at the end of the rows.

All the lint must be taken from the boll.
Slow pickers may not gather more than fifty
pounds in a day, but quick pickers will gather
three hundred pounds. One hundred pounds
is considered a fair day's work. The pickers
are paid from forty cents to one dollar for each
hundred pounds of cotton; and, since it takes
three pounds of cotton to make a pound of
cotton fiber after the seeds have been removed, you will see that cotton-picking is very

expensive for the planter. Many attempts have been made to invent machines to pick it, but none of these have succeeded.

Before the cotton can be spun into yarn, the seeds must be removed from their tiny beds. This used to be a very difficult and very expensive process; and it required one person a whole day to separate a pound of cotton. In 1792 Eli Whitney invented a machine called the cotton-gin, that does this work; and now three men with a good cotton-gin can separate ten thousand pounds in one day.

The gin is arranged with sets of teeth like combs or saws, which pull the lint off the seed. These saws revolve very fast, and, as they turn, a set of brushes takes the lint from the saw teeth and a fan blows it back into a room prepared for it. The lint is then taken to a machine which makes it up into bundles called bales. These are shipped to the great cotton-markets at Galveston, New Orleans, and Savannah, and from there to the cotton-mills. In the chapter on the New England upland we have already told you how the cotton is spun into thread and woven into cloth.

The cotton seeds were once wasted, but now

they are saved and used for many purposes. They are heated and ground and the oil is pressed out. Then they are pressed into cakes to be used as a food for animals and as a fertilizer for the land. The cotton-seed oil is burned in miners' lamps, made into soap, and used in the place of olive-oil in cooking.

Some of the States of the coastal plains, and particularly Louisiana, have many persons engaged in growing sugar-cane. The sugar-cane is a plant that looks somewhat like corn-stalks. The plants grow from three to six feet high, and in very rich soil they sometimes reach a height of ten feet.

Sugar-cane must have rich, warm, moist lands; and large areas of such lands are found in the Gulf coastal plains. The fields must be prepared very carefully for planting. They must be drained by plenty of ditches. The soil must be thoroughly plowed and harrowed to make it loose and fine. The cane is planted in rows five or six feet apart. The plowing and harrowing are done in such a way that when the field is ready the earth is heaped up in long ridges or beds. The hollows between the beds aid in the drainage of the land.

53

Sugar-cane is grown from cuttings taken from the plant itself. The sugar-cane, like the corn-stalk, is divided in joints; and at each joint there is a bud. These buds are put in the ground, and later transplanted for the new crop. The flowers rise from the stocks in tufts or plumes, and they are pink or lilac in color. In five or six months after the plants have blossomed, the golden-yellow cane stocks are ready to be cut.

The cutting is done by hand, and it is very hard work. The leaves and tops are cut off; and then the cane stocks are cut as near the ground as possible. The canes are thrown into heaps, after which they are loaded upon wagons and taken to the mills. On large plantations, tracks are laid to the fields and cars are used to haul the cane.

At the mills the cane is crushed between iron rollers. The juice flows out and is collected in large vessels. It is then boiled, skimmed, and strained, and allowed to run in broad shallow pans called coolers. Here it begins to granulate—that is, collect into small grains or particles. It is then put into sieves, and the fluid part that will not granulate drains off.

The crystals that remain in the sieves form raw or brown sugar, and the liquid that is drawn off is sold as molasses.

The white sugar that you eat is called refined sugar. Raw or brown sugar is remelted and mixed with other substances, thus removing all the impurities. Then it is poured into molds and sold as loaf-sugar. When the loaf-sugar is broken into small pieces, it is called lump-sugar; and when ground it is called granulated or powdered sugar. You probably know all these different forms of refined sugar. The drainings that come in refining sugar are sold as syrups.

Sugar is also made from a number of other plants. You may know that if a certain kind of maple-tree is tapped in the spring by boring through the bark into the wood, a sap flows out. If this sap is boiled and cooled it makes delicious maple sugar. But sugar-maple trees are not very abundant; and we must look to other plants to furnish a large part of the sugar that we eat.

The people of our country consume great quantities of sugar. The average each year for every man, woman, and child in the United

States is eighty-one pounds. That may be as much as you weigh. It takes nearly all of our great cotton crop to pay our enormous sugar bill.

Because the areas for the growing of sugar-cane are limited and so much sugar is consumed, it is now made from the juice that is squeezed from beets. Germany, Austria, Bohemia, France, and other countries of Europe have for many years grown beets for sugar; and within twenty-five years the people of our country have found that sugar-beets may be grown in the United States.

Most sugar-beets are grown in Colorado, California, and Michigan; although considerable quantities are being grown in Utah, Idaho, and Wisconsin. In the lesson on the Western plains you will learn something about irrigation. Now sugar-beets are best grown where the water-supply is under the control of the farmer—that is, where the land is irrigated; for it has been found that heavy rain, after the beets have ripened, spoils them for the purpose of making sugar.

The ground must be carefully prepared by deep plowing and fertilizing, if the soil is not rich. The seeds are planted in rows, and when they have grown a few inches high they are thinned, much as we have told you cotton-plants are thinned. The plants require a great deal of cultivation, such as hoeing and weeding.

When the plants are grown, they are dug with a beet-lifter, the tops removed, and taken to the factory. Here they are washed and cut into fine slices. The juice is soaked out of them and boiled, and the raw sugar is refined in exactly the same way as the cane-sugar.

Some Points to Remember

1. The low, flat lands along the Atlantic Ocean and the Gulf of Mexico are called coastal plains.

2. They have a moderate climate, abundant rainfall, and deep soil that is generally rich.

3. Parts of North and South Carolina, Georgia, Alabama, Mississippi, and Texas, and all of Florida and Louisiana are in the coastal plains.

4. The chief industries of the coastal plains are the growing of the cotton-plant and sugar-cane.

5. Sea-island cotton is grown on the lowest parts of the coastal plain and upland cotton on the Piedmont belt.

6. Cotton-plants grow from seeds and the fiber or lint from which cloth is made is a downy white substance that is wrapped about the seeds.

7. The separation of the lint from the seed is done by a machine called the cotton-gin.

8. Sugar-cane is grown chiefly on the moist lands of the Gulf coastal plain.

9. From the juice of the stalks we get sugar and molasses.

V.—THE CENTRAL LOWLANDS

BREAD BELT OF OUR COUNTRY: WHEAT
AND CORN

FROM the lower slopes of the Allegheny
plateau on the east, to the Rocky Mountain highland on the west—a distance of
nearly a thousand miles—are the central lowlands of our country. The land is very low;
it is level or rolling, and it is broken by few
elevations. This part of the United States is
sometimes called the Middle West.

The central lowlands are drained by the
Mississippi River and the numerous tributaries
that take their rise in the Appalachian and the
Rocky Mountain highlands. There are two
main divisions—the prairies in the East and
the Western plains, which form the foot-hills
of the Rocky Mountain highland, in the West.

In this lesson you are to read about the great
bread belt of the prairies, and in a later lesson

you will learn something about the grazing of cattle and sheep on the Western plains. The prairie lands were formerly great treeless grass plains; but to-day they contain the most valuable farm lands in our country. The soil is level and deep and rich. The winters are cold and dry, but the summers are warm and moist; and the rainfall is abundant. These facts tell you why the prairies produce vast quantities of wheat and corn and other food grains.

If you have read stories of Colonial days, you must have noticed how often corn bread and rye bread are mentioned, but how seldom wheat bread. You may also have read the story of the life of Benjamin Franklin, and recall how surprised he was when he moved from Boston to find he could buy three loaves of wheat bread for a sixpence. Wheat was then grown near Philadelphia; but in New England it was so expensive that it could only be used for pies, cakes, and biscuits.

The climate of New England and eastern New York was too cold for the growth of wheat. In the Piedmont belt and the upland regions of Pennsylvania, New Jersey, Virginia, and North Carolina, however, it did fairly well.

But there was no cheap way to carry it from place to place. This tells you why our bread supply depends upon the structural geography of our country—that is, upon the soil, the heat, and the moisture. All the grains we eat have their own notions of what they must have in order to grow. But wheat is more particular than all the others.

We did not have enough wheat bread in this country until the prairie States of the Mississippi Valley were settled, its vast stretches of rich, level land plowed, machines for handling the wheat invented, and railroads built to carry the grain to the markets where it was needed. But to-day the United States leads the world in the production of wheat.

The great wheat States—sometimes called the bread belt—of our country are in the low central plains of the upper Mississippi Valley; and the States that lead are Minnesota, North Dakota, Kansas, Nebraska, and South Dakota, although considerable quantities are grown in the narrow valleys of the Pacific coast, in Washington and California.

Two kinds of wheat are grown in our country—winter wheat and spring wheat. The winter wheat is sowed in the autumn; it lives through the winter and matures the next summer. The spring wheat is planted in the springtime and is harvested the same season. In general, spring wheat is grown in the northern part of the central lowlands and the winter wheat in the southern part.

There are three steps in the wheat industry —the sowing, the harvesting, and the marketing; and when we tell you that the States of the Mississippi Valley produce five hundred million bushels of wheat every year, you will agree that very many people must be engaged in the three branches of this industry.

The wheat-farms, as a rule, are very large, and the plowing of the fields requires hard labor. Much of the plowing is done with four horses or mules hitched to a gang-plow that turns two furrows at each trip. But on some of the largest wheat-farms they use steam and electrical plows that turn a dozen furrows at once. After the ground has been plowed and harrowed, the seed is sown in rows by a machine called a drill.

Wheat does not have to be cultivated like cotton, corn, and sugar. After the seed has

PACKING FLOUR

been sown it requires no further care until it is ripe for harvesting. It must be cut at just the right time. On the great wheat-farms of the central plains, most of the harvesting is done by machinery. The harvester is a machine that is drawn by twenty or thirty horses, or it may be drawn by an engine. It cuts a swath twenty-five feet wide and threshes the grain as it goes along.

The story of taking the wheat to market is a long one, and we cannot tell it all in this lesson. Of course it is first drawn to the nearest railroad station in wagons. Here it is stored in large buildings called elevators. It it next taken to some central wheat-market and stored in still larger elevators.

Much of the wheat is ground into flour at convenient cities in the central lowlands, and then shipped to points in the eastern part of our country or to Europe. The flour-mills at Minneapolis are among the largest in the world. This city is near the wheat-fields and it has excellent railway connections with other parts of the country. It is also not very distant from the Great Lakes, which are excellent waterways for the transportation of the flour. There are also large flour-mills at Chicago, St. Louis, and Toledo.

After wheat our great food cereal, as grains are called, is corn. It is also called maize. It was the chief food cereal of the American Indians, who were the original inhabitants of this country. And Indian corn or maize was unknown in Europe before the discovery of America by Christopher Columbus.

Corn can be grown in most parts of our country, but it does not thrive equally well in all the States. It needs rich soil, plenty of water, sunny days, and warm nights; and it must have a long season between frosts. A late frost in the spring will kill the young plants, and an early frost in the autumn will injure the golden ears.

Now all these conditions are found in the prairie States of the Mississippi Valley. This tells you that in this part of our country the soil is fertile, the rainfall is plentiful, and the nights are warm. The corn belt includes the States of Ohio, Indiana, Illinois, Iowa, Missouri, Kansas, and Nebraska. Texas also produces a large corn crop. You can easily find the States of the corn belt on a map of the United States.

Corn requires a great deal of labor. On the large corn-farms gang-plows are used. The seed is planted with machines in straight rows and the right distance apart. For corn must be cultivated. The soil must be kept loose and the weeds must be removed as often as they reappear.

Formerly the corn was cut by hand; but machines have been invented that cut the stalks and bind them into bundles. Another machines takes the husks from the ears; and still another shells and measures the corn.

Corn is used as food for animals and people and in the manufacture of starch and whiskey. Much of the corn is used near where it is grown for fattening hogs and cattle. In a later lesson on the Western plains you will read about the great herds of cattle that are raised for meat. For some time before they are sent to the markets they are fed on corn.

You probably know many of the food uses of corn for people, for you have doubtless eaten corn-cakes, johnny-cakes, mush, samp, and hominy; and you may have popped corn

65

before an open fire. Many of the breakfast foods that we eat are made from corn. Corn-cakes, johnny-cakes, and mush are made of ground corn. In hominy the hull is removed and the kernel is cooked by steam and dried. Samp is corn broken very coarsely. It was in this form that the American Indians ate the corn, because they had no way of grinding it fine.

An alcoholic drink is made of fermented corn; and as we have already said, cornstarch is a corn product. The husks and stalks of corn are fed to cattle and made into mattresses and couches. Paper and coarse bags may also be made from the leaves and stalks. Thus you see that a very great variety of uses are made of Indian corn, and you can understand why it is sometimes called the king of grains.

Some Points to Remember

1. Between the Appalachian and the Rocky Mountain highlands is a broad, low, level stretch of country called the central lowlands.

2. The lowlands are drained by the Mississippi River and its branches.

3. In the eastern and central parts of the central lowlands are the prairies; in the western part are the Western plains.

4. The prairies are level or rolling; the soil is rich and deep; the summers are warm and moist.

5. The finest farm lands in our country are found in the prairies.

6. They have sometimes been called the "bread belt" of the United States, because most of our food cereals are grown here.

6

VI.—THE GREAT LAKES

THE Great Lakes fill a hollow between the
Appalachian highland and the central lowlands. They are not so high as the highland, but they are higher than the surrounding
prairies and plains. The divide between the
lakes and the plains on the south and west is
low at most places.

The Great Lakes are five in number—Superior, Michigan, Huron, Erie, and Ontario—
and they are very large and very deep. Together they cover more square miles than the
States of the New England upland. This vast
area of water is supplied mostly by the rains
that fall on the surface of the lakes, since the
streams from their short slopes are few in number.

If you try to draw a map of the United
States, you will notice that the western half of

AMERICAN LOCK ON THE ST. MARY'S RIVER SHIP CANAL CONNECTING LAKES SUPERIOR AND HURON

the boundary between our country and Canada is a straight line and that it is easy to draw.
But the eastern half is crooked and is hard to
draw because it passes through the middle of
the Great Lakes and for some distance along
the St. Lawrence River. However, the Great
Lakes are so useful to our people that you
will be willing to have trouble with your map
when you learn more about them.

The largest and highest of the group is
Lake Superior. It is farther north and farther west and larger than the others. Its
waters flow a distance of sixty miles east
through the St. Mary's River and empty into
Lake Huron. There are rapids in the river,
and these rapids prevent steamers from going
from Lake Huron to Lake Superior. Therefore canals have been built around the rapids.
If you do not know what a canal is, ask some
one to explain it to you.

South of Lake Superior is another lake
nearly as large. It is Lake Michigan. It
also empties its waters into Lake Huron
through a broad channel known as the Straits
of Mackinac.

Lake Huron lies east of Lake Michigan. Its

waters flow through the St. Clair River, the
St. Clair Lake, and the Detroit River to Lake
Erie. There are no rapids in these streams, so
that steamships pass easily through them.

From Lake Erie the waters are carried to
Lake Ontario through the Niagara River. But
as Lake Ontario is three hundred feet lower
than Lake Erie, and the Niagara River is only
twenty-nine miles long, there is considerable
slope between the two lakes. At one place in
the river are Niagara Falls and at another a
series of rapids where the waters move with
great swiftness. In order that steamers may
pass from Lake Erie to Lake Ontario, a canal
has been built by the Canadian government
around the Falls and the rapids.

You have certainly heard of Niagara Falls,
for it is one of the most beautiful cataracts in
the world. A great volume of water falls a
distance of one hundred and sixty feet. There
are other cataracts in our country where the
water falls a greater distance than at Niagara,
but there is no other waterfall in the world
where the width is so great and where the
water is so abundant. It is these features that
make Niagara Falls one of the most beautiful

natural sights in the world. Some portions of
the water are now being used to develop
electrical power, and this power is taken to
Buffalo and other cities, where it is used to
light the streets and run factories and trolley-
cars.

In the eastern part of Lake Ontario are the
beautiful Thousand Islands with the water
threading its way among them until it unites
in one mighty stream to carry the waters of
the Great Lakes to the Atlantic Ocean. This
stream is the St. Lawrence River, which is
the great highway for Canadian trade, as well
as some of the trade of our own country.

The Great Lakes influence the climate of a
large part of our country and Canada. You
may know that large bodies of water do not
get warm or cool off as rapidly as the land.
When the waters of the Great Lakes have
become warmed during the long summer
months, they remain warm into the late
autumn. The air over the lakes mixes with
the cooler air over the land and makes it
warmer, so that the early frosts are kept off.
For this reason there are large vineyards and
peach-orchards near the Great Lakes in north-

ern Ohio, southern Michigan, and western
New York. Such fruits could not be raised in
these sections if the climate were not modified
by the waters of the Great Lakes.

When you come to study the history of the
United States, you will find that the Great
Lakes have influenced very greatly the de-
velopment and the settlement of our country.
The story of the French explorer La Salle is
one that you are certain to find full of interest.
In the early days when very little was known
about the geography of America he attempted
to build up a great fur trade with the Indians
of the Mississippi Valley; and to get his furs
to the Atlantic coast and then to Europe, he
built the first large ship that ever sailed on the
Great Lakes.

Before the time of La Salle the Indians had
sailed over the Great Lakes by means of small
boats, called canoes, which they had formed
from the trunks of trees. La Salle and his
Frenchmen carried a few tools to a place
where the city of Buffalo now stands, and
with great difficulty they built what in those
days was considered a very big ship. They
called it the *Griffin*. The Indians had never

72

seen anything like it, and they decided that La Salle must be a very great and a very powerful man.

With the *Griffin* the Frenchmen sailed over the waters of Lake Erie, through the Detroit River and Lake St. Clair and the St. Clair River to Lake Huron, and over its waters and through the Straits of Mackinac to Lake Michigan, and along the western shores of Lake Michigan to a sheltered spot that is now called Green Bay. This was the beginning of the navigation of the Great Lakes. It took La Salle and his men several weeks to make this trip.. You could make the same trip to-day in one of the big lake steamers in several days.

Since the days of La Salle and the *Griffin* many men in our own country and in Canada have used the Great Lakes as waterways for commerce. With the St. Lawrence River they form a convenient and cheap route between the central and western parts of America and the Atlantic Ocean. Since there are no high hills to separate the lake basin region from the prairies and plains of the Mississippi Valley, quantities of wheat and flour and corn and meat, as well as cattle and sheep and mineral products, are shipped to and from the different lake ports and to Europe. Fully three thousand large steamers are now regularly engaged in the lake trade.

More than half of the freight carried on the Great Lakes is iron ore. You have already read that there are rich iron-mines on the shores of Lake Superior. The ore is loaded on boats at Duluth, Superior, and other places, and taken to Toledo, Cleveland, Buffalo, and other ports on the shores of Lake Erie, where much of it is reshipped to Pittsburg and other iron-manufacturing centers in the Allegheny plateau.

Besides iron ore, the other freight shipments on the Great Lakes are pig-iron, copper, salt, logs, lumber, flour, and grain. These products are shipped from the western to the eastern ports of the lakes. The main article sent west is soft coal. Since there are so many boats to go back, and they all want to take something, they carry the soft coal at a very low rate.

Because of the cheap freight rates many great industrial cities have grown up on the shores of the Great Lakes, such as Chicago,

Toledo, Cleveland, and Buffalo. Thousands of boats unload at these lake ports every year; and since the lakes are frozen over during the winter, the wharves of these places are very busy during the spring, summer, and autumn.

The waters of the Great Lakes are clear and cool and fresh, ánd they furnish us with quantities of excellent fish. There are thousands of small boats engaged in the fishing industry; but it is dangerous business, because sudden storms are common on the lakes. Such storms rarely do harm to the large steel freight-steamers that carry iron and copper and grain and flour; but the small fishing-boats are often wrecked and the lives of many fishermen are lost every year.

Since our government has organized a Weather Bureau and established signal stations along the shores of the lakes, not nearly so many boats are wrecked and fewer lives are lost than in former years. For the government sends out warnings when storms approach, and fishermen are advised not to leave the ports. If the men are already on the lake, there is a system of signals by which the fishermen are informed of the danger.

Thus the Weather Bureau with its signal service is saving many lives and much property for the people who make their living by fishing in the Great Lakes.

Perhaps some day you will make a tour on the Great Lakes, for large and comfortable steamers carry millions of people over the lakes and to and from the different ports every year. These steamers are quite as fine and quite as comfortable as the large ocean greyhounds that sail from New York, Boston, and Philadelphia to Liverpool, Antwerp, and Hamburg.

In the northern parts of Lake Superior, as well as on the shores of Lake Huron and Lake Michigan, there are many summer resorts, with fine hotels and attractive cottages. These places have a cool and healthful climate, and thousands of people go to them every summer to escape the heat and get rest in the fresh breezes that blow from the lakes.

Some Points to Remember

1. The Great Lakes are five in number—Superior, Michigan, Huron, Erie, and Ontario.

THE GREAT LAKES

2. They fill a depression between the Appalachian highland and the central lowlands.

3. They are connected by rivers and straits and their waters find their way to the Atlantic Ocean by the St. Lawrence River.

4. They influence very greatly the climate of parts of our country.

5. They serve as cheap highways for the transportation of many of our products.

6. Their waters provide us with quantities of fish.

VII.—THE WESTERN PLAINS

GRAZING - LANDS, CATTLE AND SHEEP, AND DRY FARMING

THE gradual slopes that extend from the central lowland to the base of the Rocky Mountain highland are called the Western plains. They are crossed by many broad and shallow streams, but the rainfall is less than twenty inches a year; therefore they are slightly cultivated. They furnish excellent grazing-lands for cattle and sheep; and in recent years dry farming has been introduced in some parts of this section of our country.

The story of the life on the Western plains is the story of grazing and of the cowboys. These plains, as you have already learned, are the foot-hills of the Rocky Mountains. Fifty years ago very little was known about this section of our country, beyond the fact that it was a great desert and that it was inhabited by Indians and buffaloes.

If it were possible for you to travel all over the great Western plains, when you came back you would probably tell your schoolmates about the people you had seen and what they produced in these semi-arid regions. You would tell them that you had seen people who were engaged in raising cattle and sheep; others who worked small farms along the streams that flow from the Rocky Mountain highland; others who raise crops that are wholly or partly watered by ditches, and still others who were engaged in what is called dry farming.

If you happened to know how cattle are cared for in the eastern part of our country, you must have thought the way they did it on the Western plains very queer. In the eastern United States cattle are kept in fields with fences around them and brooks flowing through. The cows are brought to the barn at night and in the morning to be milked. In the winter they are kept in barns and sheds and fed hay and grain.

On the Western plains cattle-grazing is a

very different thing. All over this section, after the very slight rainfall in the springtime, buffalo or bunch grass grows wild in spots and patches. The hot sun dries the grass and it makes excellent food for the cattle. Countless herds of bison, or buffalo, lived on this grass for nobody knows how many centuries. About fifty years ago white men discovered that cattle could live on this grass if the buffaloes and the Indians were out of the way. The buffaloes were gradually killed, the Indians were forced to occupy lands farther west, and the cattle-raising industry of our Western plains began.

The cattle are not cared for as they are in the East, because it is not common for snow to cover the ground for weeks at a time as it does in many other parts of our country. You see, snow-clouds are not carried over the Western plains any more than rain-clouds. Besides, when snow does fall, the sweeping winds from the north blow it from the higher places and uncover the grass spots for the cattle. The cows are not milked, for the cattle are raised for beef; so there is no need to drive them home at night.

You can reason out the rest of the story for yourself. Since the grass is so scattered that it takes from ten to twenty acres to keep one animal, you see that the cattlemen must buy or rent or find for free use very large tracts of land in order to raise many cattle. Since water is scarce on the Western plains, springs must be found or wells must be dug and wind- mills set to work. The cattle must be driven to the drinking-places and to fresh pastures. The distances are too far for the men to walk, and the wild cattle of the plains can run very fast, therefore the men who keep track of the cattle — cowboys, as they are called—ride horses.

A man who goes into the cattle business must build a house by a spring or stream, where he can keep supplies, and engage a number of cowboys to look after his cattle. Nowadays nearly all the good grazing-land has been bought or rented by stockmen, and most of it has been surrounded with wire fence, so that each man's cattle may be kept on his own pastures. These pastures, or cattle ranches, as they are sometimes called, are often miles long and wide.

The work of the cowboys is to keep track of
the cattle summer and winter. After snow-
storms they must search for the animals in
hollows and cañons where they go for shelter,
and drive them to the uplands where the winds
have blown the snow from the grass. It
sometimes happens that the cowboys are
caught in blizzards and freeze to death, and
thousands of cattle are sometimes frozen or
they die of starvation because the grass is
covered with sleet.

In the spring the cowboys gather the cattle
together to find out how many have survived
the winter and to find how many calves have
been born. They are brought together again
in the fall. These semi-yearly gatherings are
called "round-ups"; and at the fall round-up
the best cattle are taken from the herds to be
sold as beef. These are driven to the nearest railroad stations, whence they are shipped
to Omaha, Kansas City, Chicago, and the
other great meat centers of our country.
Sometimes, however, they are taken to farms
in the corn belt, where they are fattened before
being slaughtered into beef.

Mention has been made of the sheep industry of the Western plains. Sheep can live with very little water and they do not require much care. For these reasons the poorer parts of the grazing-lands of the plains and the Rocky Mountain highland are made to supply us with wool for our clothes and mutton for our tables.

The sheep business is much like the cattle business, about which you have just read. Free land must be secured; a ranch-house of some kind must be provided, and men must be engaged to look after the sheep. But as the sheep are left alone much more than the cattle, the number of herders, as the men are called, is always much smaller than the number of cowboys. Indeed, one herder may take care of a thousand or more sheep. His most faithful friend is his dog, who does much of the work with great skill and fidelity.

The life of the herder is a lonely one. He is for weeks at a time alone with his dog and his sheep. He finds the best pasture that he can near a stream, and he must be constantly on the watch for such wild animals as coyotes, wolves, and mountain-lions that prey upon the young lambs. He sometimes takes with him a wagon in which to carry his food and sleep in at night.

When shearing-time arrives, the sheep are driven to places where the wool is cut off and taken to the nearest railroad stations and shipped to the factories. Sometimes the sheep are driven to the railroad stations to be sheared. Thus they are made to carry their own wool to the places from which it may be shipped. After they have been sheared some of the sheep are shipped to the great meat markets to be slaughtered for mutton.

On your imaginary trip to the Western plains you saw many farms. Some were big and some were small. The people on these farms, or ranches, as they call them, have studied carefully what will grow best on land where they have less than twenty inches of rain a year. Generally they raise grain, potatoes, and vegetables, and they raise hay and alfalfa, which they sell to the cattlemen and the sheepmen. Often they keep small herds of cattle and sheep themselves. But the life on the ranches of the Western plains is lonely, for the farms are widely separated, and it is not easy to go to church and school.

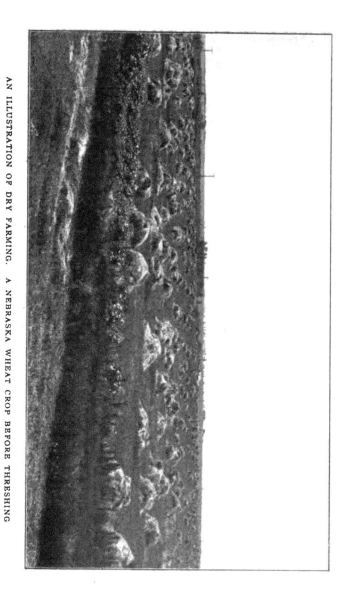

AN ILLUSTRATION OF DRY FARMING. A NEBRASKA WHEAT CROP BEFORE THRESHING

But the newest and strangest thing that you might have seen on your visit to the Western plains was what is called dry farming. As this was begun only a few years ago, probably most of your schoolmates have never heard of it. In semi-arid regions, where the annual rainfall is not more than twenty inches a year, grain could be raised if only the water was saved.

Dry farming means that men have found a way to save this water so that it may be used for growing useful things. It is natural for water to find its way up to the surface of the soil. You know if you put one end of a towel in a pitcher of water and hang up the other end, the water will follow along the threads of the towel up to the top. Now in much the same way, if particles of soil are packed close enough together, the water below will climb up along the soil particles to the surface and evaporate, or be lost in the air.

This is just what the farmer does not want to happen. The problem, then, is to keep the water from passing off into the air. It was noticed on the Western plains, and in other places where it does not rain for a long time, that the dust gets very deep in the roads and that it is always damp under the dust. The water does not come up through the dust because the particles are not close enough together so they can act like the threads of the towel.

What the farmer must do is to cover his field with a thick layer of very fine earth. Such layers are called mulch. The land is plowed very deep, and where the soil is hard it takes a machine plow to do this. It is allowed to lie until the winter's snow and the spring rains have soaked into it. Then the soil is pulverized very fine and the seeds are sowed deep with a drill.

Thousands of acres in western Kansas, Nebraska, and Wyoming, and other States in our country, have already been made to yield crops of grain, hay, and other food plants; and, if our people continue to develop dry farming, the Western plains will soon be more thickly settled with homes, and the life on the ranches will be less lonely than in the past. When you come to study about Africa and Australia, and other countries where the rainfall is slight, you will learn more about dry farming.

THE WESTERN PLAINS

Some Points to Remember

1. The Western plains are the gradual slopes between the central lowlands and the Rocky Mountain highland.

2. Their lands are semi-arid because they get an annual rainfall of less than twenty inches.

3. Bunch or buffalo grass springs up after the slight rainfall, and this furnishes food for great herds of cattle and sheep.

4. Farm-houses are scattered, and only along the river bottoms has much attempt been made at agriculture.

5. Some progress, however, has been made since the introduction of dry farming.

VIII.—THE ROCKY MOUNTAIN HIGH-LAND

MINING OF GOLD, SILVER, LEAD, AND COPPER

IN the western part of our country is the Rocky Mountain highland. It is one of the largest and highest plateau sections in the world, and it extends the entire length of the North American continent. Hence, it is sometimes called the primary highland of North America. The States of Montana, Idaho, Wyoming, Colorado, Utah, Nevada, New Mexico, and Arizona are in this section. They are called the Plateau States of America, because they belong to this elevated plateau region.

The Rocky Mountains form the eastern and the Sierra Nevada and Cascade Mountains the western walls or borders of the highland; and between the two great ranges there are numerous mountain ridges and peaks and interven-

IRRIGATION IN A COLORADO PEACH ORCHARD

ing plateaus and basins. Most of the highland is more than a mile above sea-level, and some of the peaks are nearly three miles high. The eastern slopes of the Rocky Mountains and the western slopes of the Sierra Nevadas are steep; but the inner slopes toward the basins and plateaus of the highland are more gradual.

Many of the sharp, narrow ranges of the highland are the upturned edges of blocks of the earth's crust, and here are found the rich deposits of gold, silver, copper, and lead. The high Sierra Nevada Mountains on the western edge take the moisture from the damp, warm winds that come from the Pacific Ocean. Hence, rainfall is very slight, and vegetation is scarce.

Many parts of the Rocky Mountain highland get only ten inches of rain a year, and there are parts that have an annual rainfall of less than one inch. You will remember that in the New England upland the annual rainfall is from thirty-five to fifty inches; in the prairies from thirty to forty inches, and in parts of the coastal plains from forty to sixty inches.

In most parts of the highland agriculture can only be carried on by means of irrigation.

89

The elevation of the Plateau States being so very great, the winters are cold and the snow is often very deep. But the rocks of the mountains contain quantities of rich minerals, and large herds of cattle and sheep are grazed in the mountain valleys of the highland.

Most of the cities and towns are near the gold, silver, copper, and lead mines. But the highland is very thinly inhabited. The eight Plateau States contain seven times more square miles of area than the six States of the New England upland, but altogether their population is less than that of the small State of Massachusetts.

The Rocky Mountain highland is the home of many of the Indians of our country. They live on land set aside for them by the government and cultivate small tracts of land, raise horses, cattle, and sheep, and make baskets, blankets, and beads. Formerly great herds of buffalo and other wild animals roamed over the plateaus of the highland, but they have largely disappeared. Only in the Yellowstone National Park, where they are protected by the government, does one find wild animals in considerable number.

There are three large plateaus in the part of the Rocky Mountain highland that is in the United States. They are the Colorado plateau, the Great Basin, and the Columbia plateau. The Colorado plateau is composed of high peaks and rugged ridges in Colorado and parts of Utah and Arizona. Three mountain peaks—Pike's Peak, the Mountain of the Holy Cross, and Blanco Peak—are each more than 14,000 feet high. Between the high mountain ranges of the plateau there are great mountain valleys called parks. Some of these parks are as large as the State of Massachusetts.

The Colorado River drains the plateau. It is formed by the junction of the Grand and the Green Rivers, and flows southwest to the Gulf of California. As it flows over the weaker and softer rocks of the plateau, it has worn deep gorges. The Grand Cañon of the Colorado River is the largest cañon in the world. Where it cuts through the rim of the plateau, for a distance of two hundred miles, it has worn a channel from half a mile to a mile deep. This is one of the most picturesque natural sights in our country.

The Great Basin is an elevated plateau more than a mile above sea-level. It is inclosed by the high Sierra Nevada Mountains on the west and the Wasatch Mountains on the east. It is less rugged than the Colorado plateau, and most of the country is desert in character. Forests are absent, except on the California side of the Sierra Nevada Mountains, and sage-brush and bunch-grass are the chief forms of vegetation. For many months each year the sky is without a cloud, and not a drop of rain falls. Many of the valleys, however, are broad and deep, and might be made into artificial lakes for purposes of irrigation.

Over considerable parts of the Great Basin the rainfall is less than an inch a year, and the rivers lose themselves in the deserts and the lakes dry up during the summer months. The two principal rivers of the Great Basin are the Carson and the Humboldt. The Carson takes its rise on the eastern slope of the Sierra Nevada Mountains, and it has a length of one hundred and twenty-five miles. Its waters spread out in the Carson desert and evaporate. After flowing for nearly three hundred miles, through a treeless part of the Great Basin, the Humboldt River expands and forms the Humboldt Lake. These streams and lakes are not pure, but contain quantities of salt and other mineral matter.

There is, however, one beautiful fresh-water lake on the western rim of the Great Basin. This is Lake Tahoe, the "gem of the Sierras." It is the highest lake in our country, being more than a mile above sea-level, and is surrounded by steep mountains that are covered with trees. It is twenty-one miles long, twelve miles broad, and very deep. Its water is pure and clear, and the lake contains trout and other fish. Unlike most of the other lakes of the Great Basin, it has an outlet. Its overflow of water escapes by a rocky gorge through the Truckee River to Winnemucca Lake. Tahoe is fed by many swift streams that take their rise among the snow-fields of the surrounding mountain ridges and peaks.

North of the Great Basin is the Columbia plateau, which is drained by the Columbia River and its numerous branches. Here the rainfall is greater than on other parts of the highland and rivers are more abundant. Some of the highest peaks in the Cascade are extinct volcanoes, and thousands of miles are covered with lava. Where the lava has decayed, an excellent soil has been formed. Minerals have been carried near the surface by streams that have been heated by contact with volcanic rocks. As the waters cooled near the surface, the mineral substances were deposited and veins of metals were formed.

The highest part of the Columbia plateau is occupied by the Yellowstone National Park, a reservation set apart by the government of the United States for a public pleasure ground. With the forest reserves, the park contains 5,500 square miles, or about the area of the State of Connecticut. The average altitude of the park is about a mile and a half. There are twenty-four peaks in the park more than two miles high. The rainfall is greater and streams are more numerous than in most other parts of the Rocky Mountain highland. Some deep valleys have been cut by the streams in the surface lava-beds.

.One of the most interesting and beautiful is the cañon of the Yellowstone River. The Yellowstone enters the southeastern corner of the park and soon flows into the Yellow-stone Lake. Shortly after it leaves the lake it falls over a precipice one hundred and ten feet high and then through a narrow gorge of yellow, red, and green rocks, known as the Yellowstone Cañon.

The park is richly forested with black pine, balsam, and fir trees; and as the government does not allow guns carried in the park and wild animals killed, there are many elk, moose, deer, antelope, bear, beaver, and mountain-sheep.

There are more than three thousand hot springs and geysers in the Columbia plateau; and the largest of these, more than seventy in number, are in the Yellowstone National Park. These geysers and hot springs are due to vol-canic heat still present under the surface of the lava-beds of the plateau. They spout hot water into the air many feet. The Old Faith-ful geyser spouts a column of hot water one hundred and twenty-five feet high every hour; and the Giant geyser, which is less regular, sends up a column two hundred feet high.

The Rocky Mountain highland contains most of the gold, silver, copper, and lead mines in our country. As you may know, gold is regarded as the most beautiful and the most precious metal; although you have learned in the lesson on the Allegheny plateau that iron is more useful than gold or silver. But gold is very valuable because it is scarce and because it is easily worked. It is not affected by the air, and it is not readily eaten by the common acids.

The chief uses of gold are for money, ornaments, and jewelry. Pure gold is soft, and it must be mixed with other metals to harden it. Such a mixture is called an alloy. Copper is the chief alloy used with gold.

Gold may also be hammered in thin leaves and used as a gilding for dishes, picture-frames, and furniture, and gold-leaf is also much used in the decoration and lettering of book covers. But the chief use of gold in all the countries of the world is for money.

The United States is the largest gold-producing country in the world, and most of the gold of our country comes from the mines in the Rocky Mountain highland. Gold is found in many kinds of rocks, but chiefly in quartz. As the rocks tumble away by the action of rain

and frost, the grains of gold that they contain
are washed down by the streams into river-
beds. The gold is obtained by washing the
gravel in pans.

More often the metal is obtained by turn-
ing powerful streams of water against gold-
bearing gravel banks; and the gold being
heavier than the gravel, the latter is carried
away. Mines where gold is thus obtained are
called placer mines. We have already said
that gold is heavier than gravel. As it finds
its way to the gravel-beds, it settles in holes
or pockets. In placer mines, the upper layers
of gravel are dug away and the largest lumps
of gold—called nuggets—are found in pockets.
A nugget of gold once found in a placer mine in
Australia weighed two hundred and thirty-
three pounds.

Most of the gold in the Rocky Mountain
highland is found in quartz or other hard
rocks. After the gold-bearing quartz rocks
have been mined, they are crushed and smelted. At the stamping - mills the ores are
crushed into a fine powder, and at the smelting-
mills, by the aid of mercury, the gold is separated from the quartz grains and other earthy

substances. The pure gold-dust may be melted and run into molds, forming solid masses
called bullion. Gold-dust and bullion are
alloyed with copper or silver and made into
money or jewelry.

About four-fifths of the gold of the world
is made into money. It is made into money
only at mints that are controlled by the
government; but a miner may send his gold-
dust or bullion to a mint, where it is made
into coin without charge. The United States
has mints for the coining of gold into money at
Philadelphia, New Orleans, Denver, and San
Francisco.

Silver, another valued metal, is found in
great quantities in the Rocky Mountain highland. The five States of Colorado, Montana,
Utah, Nevada, and Arizona produce most of
the silver of our country and we are the largest
silver-producing country in the world. Silver
is found in more places and in greater quantities than gold. It is never found entirely
pure, but is mixed with gold, copper, lead, and
mercury. About half the silver of the United
States comes from lead ores.

The ores are mined and crushed into powder

by machines, after which mercury is mixed with the powder. This is heated in iron vessels, and the mercury and other foreign substances pass off as vapor and the silver is left in the vessel. Silver is harder than gold and it takes a beautiful polish, but it tarnishes more easily than gold. Like gold it is easily hammered into thin sheets and drawn into threads.

Its uses are varied, but pure silver is too soft to wear well, and it is therefore hardened by mixing with copper. It is too common and its value changes too frequently to be used extensively for money. Therefore less than a sixth of the silver that is produced is used for coinage purposes. Its largest use is in jewelry, although it is also used in the manufacture of tableware, indelible inks, hair-dyes and medicine, and in photography.

Mexico is the second largest silver-producing country. Together with the United States, it produces more than half the silver of the world. Bolivia is third; Australia and New Zealand are fourth, and Germany is fifth.

Copper, one of the first metals known to man, is also an important mineral product of

the Rocky Mountain highland. Outside of
the Lake Superior region, where copper is
found nearly pure, most of the copper of the
world is found in combination with other
mineral substances. More than half of the
copper of the world comes from the United
States; and the copper-mines near Butte and
Anaconda in Montana are our chief sources.
Arizona, Michigan, and Utah also rank high in
the production of copper ores.

Copper takes a fine polish; it is easily drawn
into wire and hammered into sheets; and, because of its hardness, it is much used as an
alloy in mixture with gold, silver, and other
metals. It is an excellent conductor of electricity; and, with the introduction of trolley-
cars run by electricity, copper wire is much in
demand. Much copper wire is also used for
telegraph and telephone lines.

Copper is alloyed—that is, mixed—with
tin to make bronze and bell-metal; with zinc
to make brass; and with nickel and zinc
to make German silver. Copper plates are
widely used in roofing, covering the bottoms
of ships, and in engraving. Copper is also
used in the making of blue-vitriol, in the color-

COPPER SMELTERS IN MICHIGAN

ing of glass, and in the dyes in printing calico. Many ornaments are made from copper, and copper sheets are cut in fine layers and used as a veneer in costly furniture.

You have already been told that lead is found in combination with ores that yield gold and silver. Hence the Rocky Mountain highland, that ranks so high in connection with the production of these metals, must also take high rank in the production of lead. The principal ore of lead is galena, and Colorado ranks first in the production of this metal. Leadville, Pueblo, and Cripple Creek are not only great silver - producing cities, but also lead in the production of lead.

Lead is easily melted and drawn into sheets. Hence it is widely used for gas-pipe and for plumbing purposes. It is easily soldered and it does not rust as readily as many other soft metals. Its use in the arts is great, as in the manufacture of paints, shot, type for printing, and cannon-balls.

The five leading lead-producing States in our country are Colorado, Missouri, Idaho, Utah, and Montana. Spain leads in the production of lead, and the United States

ranks second; Germany is third, and Mexico
fourth

Some Points to Remember

1. The Rocky Mountain highland is one of
the largest elevated regions in the world. It
is a part of the primary highland of North
America.

2. It includes the eight Plateau States—viz.,
Montana, Idaho, Wyoming, Colorado, Nevada, New Mexico, and Arizona.

3. The highland is formed by two great
mountain ranges—the Rocky Mountains and
the Sierra Nevada Mountains.

4. The rainfall of the highland is slight;
agriculture is not important, but the mountains contain quantities of gold, silver, copper, and lead.

5. The three large plateaus of the highland
are the Colorado plateau, the Great Basin,
and the Columbia plateau.

IX.—THE CALIFORNIA VALLEY

FRUIT ORCHARDS, VINEYARDS, AND FORESTS

IF you were to go from the Atlantic to the Pacific Ocean by train, say from New York to San Francisco, you could get a very good notion of the geography of the United States. It would take less than six days to make the journey by an express train; and during that time you would have crossed the narrow Atlantic coastal plain, the Piedmont belt, the Allegheny plateau, the prairies of the Mississippi Valley, the Western plains, the Rocky Mountain highland, and the California Valley. If you had kept your eyes open, you would probably know a great deal about the structure of the different sections of our country that you have read about in this book, as well as something about the people and what they do to provide for their needs and comforts.

If you cannot make the journey by an express train, perhaps you will make it in imagination, since you want to reach the Pacific coast to study the beautiful valleys of California and Oregon and Washington, and learn some things about the fruit orchards and the vineyards and the forests of the Pacific coast.

Starting at sea-level in New York, you cross the low Atlantic coastal plain and the slightly higher Piedmont belt in New Jersey and eastern Pennsylvania, until you reach Harrisburg. Your train soon begins to climb the low, broken ridges of the old Appalachian Mountains, and you find yourself on the Allegheny plateau and in the heart of the coal and oil fields and the center of the iron and steel industries about which you have already read.

From Pittsburg, you descend the gradual slopes of the plateau to the prairies; and cross Indiana, Illinois, and Iowa. At Omaha you are at the lowest point in the great central plains of the United States, for you are on a branch of the Mississippi River; and you have already learned that the low plains and the prairies are drained by this mighty stream.

You continue to see rolling prairies with cultivated grain - fields and prosperous - looking
farmsteads as you cross the State of Nebraska.

At a place called Grand Island your train
begins to climb a little. On either side of you
are stretches of grassy plain, isolated farm-
houses, and large droves of cattle; and ahead
of you in the distance a range of high, rocky
mountains. You rightly guess that you are
crossing the Western plains.

Your train continues to climb, and the slope
grows less gradual. Soon you find yourself in
Colorado among mountain ranges and passes
that are more than a mile and a half above
Omaha and the cities of the prairies through
which your train has just passed. You guess
again, and this time that you are on the eastern rim of the great Rocky Mountain highland,
about which you read in the previous lesson.
At Denver and Leadville you see great smoke-
stacks that you are told belong to the mills
where gold and silver are smelted and refined.

You leave these cities miles behind and
descend several thousand feet; you are still
among high mountains—you find that you are
a mile above the level of the sea. But that is

still very high, probably much higher than you had ever been before you started on this tour across our country.

You cross the States of Utah and Nevada through a plateau-like region that you are told is the Great Basin and that it was once known as the American Desert. At Reno in western Nevada your train begins to climb again, until you find yourself on the summit of snow-covered mountains that are nearly two miles above the level of the sea. This time you guess that you have reached the Sierra Nevada Mountains, the western rim of the great Rocky Mountain highland.

From the crest of the high Sierras, your train descends rapidly through forests of timber to Sacramento, and you are told that you have reached the California Valley; and that you are only ninety miles from the Pacific Ocean. As you have been told that the valley is narrow and long, and you see by the map that Sacramento is near the center, you expect to see the ocean very soon. Ahead of you, however, you observe a range of hills. This is the Coast Range that separates the California Valley from the Pacific coast: for if this range were not here, we would speak of the Piedmont belt or the coastal plain of the Pacific coast, and not of the California Valley.

Having reached San Francisco and seen the beautiful Pacific Ocean, you will linger long enough to study the geography of the long and narrow valley that is famous for its orchards and vineyards.

The California Valley is a depression between the Sierra Nevada and the Cascade Mountains on the east and the Coast Range on the west. It is six hundred and fifty miles long and has an average width of about forty miles. The northern part of the valley is drained by the Sacramento River, and the southern part by the San Joaquin River. The lowest part of the valley is in the middle, where the two rivers meet. At this point there is a break in the Coast Range. This break is at the point where the city of San Francisco is located, and it is called the Golden Gate.

The western slopes of the Sierra Nevada and the Cascade Mountains are well watered. They are in the path of the prevailing western winds; and the coast ranges are not high enough to take their moisture as they come from the Pacific Ocean. Many streams, therefore, take their rise on the abrupt slopes of the Sierras and the Cascades, and empty into the Sacramento and the San Joaquin rivers at different points in the California Valley.

These streams have worn deep cañons into the sides of the steep slopes of the Sierra Nevada Mountains; and in spite of the fact that the rocks are very hard, the constant action of the rapid currents has dug channels that are hundreds and thousands of feet deep, through which plunge the streams that are fed by the perpetual snows on the upper slopes of the big Sierras. On the lower slopes of the mountains, the cañons often widen into small valleys. Such a gorge is the famous Yosemite Valley.

The valleys in the northern part of the Pacific coast have plenty of rain—in some places eighty inches a year or more; but in the great California Valley it is much less; and in the smaller valleys in southern California it is sometimes not more than ten or fifteen inches a year. Now crops cannot be grown, and therefore people and animals cannot get a living, on land that receives less than ten inches of rain a year; and most food plants cannot be grown unless there is more than twenty inches.

On the Western plains, in the Rocky Mountain highland, and in parts of central and southern California, the rainfall is less than twenty inches. In the lesson on the Western plains we told you something of the way crops were raised by dry farming; and we mentioned that in some places crops were raised by means of irrigation.

When not enough rain falls, or when it all comes during three or four months of the winter—as it does in California—water must be carried to the land. This is called irrigation.

Land is irrigated in a number of different ways. One of the easiest is to dig a ditch so as to lead the water from a stream along the side of a field. Little gates are made in the sides of the ditch, and when they are opened the water runs down over the field. The trouble with this plan is that most streams are lower than the fields; so, if you made a ditch, the water would not run up onto the land.

Irrigation is therefore easiest in a hilly coun-

try, or where there is considerable slope to the
land, as on the Western plains, in the Rocky
Mountain highland, and on the slopes of the
California Valley. A dam is made across a
stream up in the hills, thus forming a reservoir
or pond. Ditches are made from the reservoir
down the hillsides to the different farms where
the water is wanted.

If a farmer in a dry country is lucky enough
to have a spring upon a hillside, he can dig a
pond below his spring and make ditches from
it to any part of his farm. Sometimes wells
are drilled and water is pumped from the
ground, but this is very expensive.

In most places in California irrigation is
carried on by big companies on a large scale.
They build great reservoirs that are really
small lakes. They dig miles of ditches and
build walls of stone or concrete. In this way
water is brought from far up in the mountains
and carried to distant places. The water
companies charge the farmers and fruit-grow-
ers a certain rate for water, just as in cities a
rate is charged for the water that is used in
homes.

Thousands of farms have been made to grow

paying crops which would otherwise have remained waste land. Thousands of families have comfortable homes and beautiful grounds which would not have been possible if each land-owner had been obliged to bring water for himself. The rich orchards of oranges and lemons, the big groves of English walnuts and almonds, and the vast grape vineyards of California have all been made possible by irrigation.

Most of the fine, large, yellow oranges that you buy in the market and at the fruit-stands are grown in California. All through the California Valley, and particularly in the southern part of the State, there are many orange groves; and the groves are always beautiful. In the late springtime the trees are covered with pure white flowers that are very fragrant and very beautiful. In the late summer they are loaded with great green apples that become golden in the late autumn and early winter. And even in the late winter and early springtime, before the trees have blossomed, an orange orchard is a handsome sight, for the trees are evergreen—that is, they are covered with green leaves throughout the year.

The orange does best on low, fertile land that is free of frost and easily irrigated. The trees reach a height of from twenty to thirty feet. The orchards are kept free of all grass and weeds, and the moisture is supplied to the roots by water that is brought to the groves in irrigating ditches and emptied in pools at the base of the trees. The oranges begin to ripen in December, although the picking season continues until April. The longer the fruit hangs on the trees, the sweeter it gets. Oranges must be taken from the trees by hand. Men and women, and sometimes Chinamen, for many Chinamen live in California, cut the stems from the branches and place the fruit in sacks or cloth-lined baskets.

The oranges are taken to packing-rooms, where they are first sorted and graded. After each orange has been wrapped in tissue-paper, they are put in boxes of uniform size. You can put only ninety-six of the largest oranges in one of these boxes, but it takes two hundred and fifty-two of the smallest fruit to fill a box of the same size. Most of the boxes, however, contain from one hundred and eighty to two hundred oranges.

The first orange-trees were brought to America by the Mission Fathers and planted at San Gabriel (near Pasadena), San Diego, Santa Barbara, and other places where they established missions in California. The Valencia orange, a late Spanish variety that keeps well, was first grown; but to-day the large . Washington navels, the Mediterranean sweets, the blood oranges, so called because of their dark-red juice, the mandarins, or kid-glove oranges, and many other kinds are grown in the orchards of California.

Most of the oranges that are grown are eaten as fruit, but some of them are made into marmalade and preserves; and an oil is made from the blossoms that is used in making cologne and other perfumes. The orange wood is very valuable, because it is hard and close-grained and takes a high polish.

California has nearly as many lemon as orange orchards. Lemons belong to the same family as oranges, and at a distance lemon orchards look much like orange orchards. But lemons do not require so much heat to ripen; they are not so perishable as oranges, and they can be marketed at any season of the year.

Lemons must be quite as carefully picked as oranges. They are sent to cool store-houses, where they are sorted and boxed and shipped to different parts of the country as they are needed. Besides the use that is made of them as a cooling drink, lemons are used in making various acids; and an oil is made from the peel that is used in medicine.

The apricot, a fruit much like the peach, is also grown in California. But it is very perishable, and must be used a few days after it ripens. Much of the California apricot crop is dried; some of it is canned, and some is candied—that is, preserved in sugar. There are many other fruits in California that are found only in warm countries, such as figs, nectarines, guavas, pomegranates, and limes.

Besides these tropical and subtropical fruits, there are great orchards of peaches, cherries, and plums in California, and apples and pears are grown in Oregon and Washington. The largest and finest fruit that you see in the markets comes from the Pacific coast; and the best dried and canned fruit that you

114

buy at the stores is grown and canned or dried in California, Washington, or Oregon. The large, fine prunes that you sometimes have for your breakfast are plums that have been grown and dried in California.

Another fruit that is extensively cultivated in California is the olive. Like the orange and the lemon, the olive is an evergreen tree. The leaves are much like those of the willow—dull green above and whitish underneath. The flowers are small and white, and appear in clusters. The trees grow to be twenty or thirty feet high and they live for hundreds of years. The wood makes very valuable lumber, but the fruit is the most useful part of the tree.

There are two varieties of olives—the large green, sometimes called the Spanish olive, and the small purple olive. Olives are eaten as a relish, and an excellent oil is made from the fruit. Those that are to be eaten are pickled in a brine of lime-water. The olives that are to be made into oil are pressed into a pulp, much as is done with apples when they are made into cider. The olive-oil that you may have eaten on your salad is simply the juice of the olive fruit. The oil is much used for cooking purposes, and in some parts of southern Europe the people spread it on their bread in the place of butter. It is also burned in lamps, and the best soaps are made of it.

Fruits are not the only good things that California gives us. It is sometimes called the Italy of America because its climate and fruits are so much like those of Italy; and not only does it produce oranges and lemons and other subtropical fruits as good or better than those grown in Italy, but it also produces English walnuts, almonds, and other nuts that we used to get entirely from Italy and the warm countries of southern Europe.

The English walnut-trees are planted in rows like orchard fruit-trees, and they grow to a height of from sixty to eighty feet and have great, spreading branches. Like the orange and lemon trees, they must be irrigated. Walnut orchards begin to bear nuts when they are six or seven years old, and they continue bearing for many years.

It is not very difficult to gather the nuts when they are ripe, and children often help the Chinese and Japanese workmen. In some districts in California the school-children have a "walnut vacation" so that they may help to gather the ripened nuts. After the nuts have been gathered they are dried and hulled and bleached. The bleaching gives them a lighter color. More than a thousand car-loads of English walnuts are shipped from California every year.

Almonds are also grown in California. They do well in semi-arid sections that are well drained and where the climate is warm; but, like the oranges and the lemons and the English walnuts, they must be irrigated. The trees grow only half as tall as the English walnuts. They have beautiful white blossoms that resemble those you may have seen on peach-trees in the spring.

When the nuts are ripe the hulls are removed and they are dried ready for shipment to the markets. California produces more than five thousand tons of almonds each year; but so many almonds are eaten in our country that we buy in addition nearly a million dollars' worth yearly from Italy and the warm countries of the Old World. Most almonds are eaten as nuts, but some of them are pressed for their oil, which is used in making candies and perfumery.

Hundreds of thousands of acres of land in California are covered by vineyards. Single fields sometimes contain a thousand acres; and there is a vineyard near Los Angeles that contains five thousand acres. The California grapes are trained to grow as stubby shrubs, and not allowed to trail as vines. They are trimmed every winter, and the stumps, which are often ten inches thick, are allowed to reach a height of not more than two or three feet. New branches spring from the stump every year, upon which great clusters of grapes grow. A single cluster may sometimes weigh five pounds. Seen at a distance a California vineyard looks much like an orchard of small trees.

Grapes are grown in California for wine and raisins; for both purposes warmth and sunshine are necessary; and the warm climate and the constant sunshine for many months during the summer have made the wine and raisin industries very profitable in many parts of the State. Wine is made by pressing the juice from the grape and allowing it to ferment—that is, to change from grape-juice into

an alcoholic drink. When the grapes are ripe
they are cut from the branches, loaded on
wagons, and taken to the wineries.

Raisins are simply dried grapes. The best
raisins are made from white Muscatel and
Malaga grapes. The bunches of grapes are
cut from the branches, spread out thinly on
trays made of laths, and left in the sun to dry.
From time to time they are turned over, that
all the grapes on the bunch may get the sun,
since the bunches are very large.

As you know, grapes contain much sweet
juice. This sweet juice is really water and
sugar. The warm sun takes the water from
the grape, but it leaves behind the sugar.
After the grapes have been cured by being
exposed to the sun for a couple of weeks, they
are taken to a dark room and allowed to
sweat for ten days. This causes the very
little moisture that remains in the center of
the grapes to soften the dried outer skins and
the stems.

The next step is to sort and pack the raisins.
This work is done very largely by women and
Chinamen. The large perfect bunches are
packed in boxes by themselves. They bring

the highest prices. . The imperfect bunches are packed in other boxes; and the loose raisins, after the stems have been removed, are boxed and sold for cooking purposes. The finest California raisins are produced near Fresno, in the southern portion of the San Joaquin Valley.

You have already read that the steep slopes of the Sierra Nevada and the Cascade Mountains separate the valleys of the Pacific coast from the Rocky Mountain highland. You have also learned that the western slopes of these mountains are well watered by the warm, moist winds that come from the Pacific Ocean. As a result, these abrupt slopes are forested with cone-bearing trees.

Midway between the lowest part of the valley and the summit of the high Sierra Nevada ridges we find the sugar-pine, the most valued of all the pine-trees because of its whiteness and fine grain. It is a tall, slender tree, often reaching a height of two hundred feet and a diameter of twelve feet.

Still higher up the slopes are found scattered groves of "big trees." These are the oldest and the largest trees found anywhere in the world. The family name of the "big trees" is *Sequoia*, and they belong to the fir variety of trees. Some of them grow as high as three hundred and fifty feet and have a diameter of thirty feet. One of the big trees requires twenty-two men with finger-tips to tips to reach round it. In another of these trees a hole ten feet square has been cut, through which a loaded stage-coach can drive.

On the Coast Range in California are vast forests of another kind of *Sequoia* known as the redwood. This is one of the most valuable lumber products of the Pacific coast. It is much more abundant than the "big trees," and it has the same rich, dark-red color. It also takes a high polish; and the absence of pitch and rosin enables it to resist fire.

There are several fine valleys on the Pacific coast north of the California Valley. The Rogue, the Umpqua, and the Willamette valleys are in Oregon. They lie between the Cascade Mountains on the east and the Coast Range on the west. The Willamette Valley is the longest. It extends north and south for a distance of nearly two hundred miles. There are fine orchards and rich grain-fields in the

Rogue and the Umpqua valleys. Some of the finest apples that we buy at the fruit-stands are grown in these valleys.

The Willamette Valley is composed of rich, rolling prairie lands. The rainfall is abundant and the climate is moderate. Great quantities of hops, fruit, barley, wheat, and other grains are produced in the valley. The hop-fields of the Willamette Valley are among the largest in the world. The hops are supported on poles and grow to a height of twenty feet. The flowers are dried for use in making beer, yeast, and medicine.

The Willamette joins the Columbia River near Portland. In the lesson on the Rocky Mountain highland you learned some things about the Columbia plateau and the Columbia River. One thing that you learned was that thousands of miles were covered with lava— that is, melted rock material that had been thrown from volcanoes or issued from fissures in the surface of the plateau. We also told you that when the lava was decayed it made excellent soil.

Now the Columbia River, as it leaves the higher regions of the plateau to break through the mountain ranges and empty its waters into the Pacific Ocean, has widened into a river valley in southern Washington. The Columbia is joined by numerous streams from the plateau that have also formed river valleys. In these river valleys the lava has disintegrated — that is, it has broken up into little pieces. Disintegrated lava makes very rich soil. We find, therefore, in the Columbia Valley, as well as in the Yakima Valley and other river valleys that join the Columbia, some of the richest farm and orchard lands in the world. Grain and fruit are grown in abundance; and the apples of Washington, like those of Oregon, are the finest that are produced in our country.

The Puget Sound Basin is in the northwestern part of our country, in the State of Washington. It is covered with a rich soil, and the rainfall is from sixty to seventy inches a year. There are many farms in the basin, where wheat, barley, and hay are grown, and many apple, plum, and peach orchards. Seattle and Tacoma, two great trade centers in the northwestern part of the United States, are situated on Puget Sound.

On the western slopes of the Cascade Mountains in Oregon and Washington there are great forests, similar to those found in the Sierras. There is plenty of rain, for the clouds come from the Pacific, and the mountains make them give up their moisture. The Cascades are much better watered than the Sierras. The land slopes so that it is well drained, and the great mountains themselves protect the trees from the terrible arctic winds that come from the northeast.

While the trees on the slopes of the Cascade Mountains are not so large as the "big trees" on the slopes of the Sierras, they are so much larger than the trees in most other parts of the country that you would be pretty certain to call them giants. Many of the shingles, laths, and boards used in our country come from these forests. The Cascade slopes in Washington and Oregon produce more lumber than any other section of our country; and Seattle and Tacoma in Washington and Portland in Oregon are the great centers for the lumber trade.

Some Points to Remember

1. The California Valley is a depression between the Sierra Nevada and the Cascade

Mountains on the east and the Coast Range on the west.

2. It extends a distance of six hundred and fifty miles along the Pacific coast, and is drained by the Sacramento and San Joaquin rivers.

3. There are deep cañons in the slopes that extend from the Sierras to the California Valley.

4. There are rich orchards of oranges and lemons, big groves of English walnuts and almonds, and vast grape vineyards in California.

5. There are also fine orchards and rich farm lands in the river valleys of Oregon and Washington.

6. On the slopes of the Sierra Nevada and Cascade Mountains there are great forests of cone-bearing trees.

INDEX

INDEX

THE END